fro
Journey

frodo's journey

Discovering the Hidden Meaning of *The Lord of the Rings*

Joseph Pearce

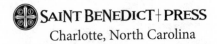

SAINT BENEDICT + PRESS

Charlotte, North Carolina

Cover design by Caroline Kiser.

Cover image by Eric Edwards.

Unless otherwise stated, the Scripture excerpts in *Frodo's Journey* are from the Douay Rheims Bible.

Cataloging-in-Publication data on file with the Library of Congress.

Paperbound ISBN 978-1-61890-675-5
ePub ISBN 978-1-61890-730-1

Published in the United States by Saint Benedict Press, LLC
PO Box 410487
Charlotte, NC 28241
www.SaintBenedictPress.com

Printed and bound in the United States of America.

For Stephen Brady:
hobbit, friend, and traveling companion

CONTENTS

CHAPTER 1

"A FUNDAMENTALLY RELIGIOUS AND CATHOLIC WORK"

The Lord of the Rings is of course a fundamentally religious and Catholic work; unconsciously so at first, but consciously in the revision. That is why I have not put in, or have cut out, practically all references to anything like "religion," to cults or practices, in the imaginary world. For the religious element is absorbed into the story and the symbolism.

—J. R. R. Tolkien to Robert Murray, S.J.[1]

As for any inner meaning or "message," it has in the intention of the author none. It is neither allegorical nor topical. . . . I cordially dislike allegory in all its manifestations, and always have done so since I grew old and wary enough to detect its presence.

—J. R. R. Tolkien[2]

There is a mystery at the heart of *The Lord of the Rings* that continues to baffle and confuse the critics. Is it

1

"a fundamentally religious and Catholic work," as Tolkien claimed in a letter to his Jesuit friend, Father Robert Murray, in December 1953, or is it, as he claimed in the foreword to the second edition of *The Lord of the Rings*, devoid of any intentional meaning or "message"? If Tolkien dislikes allegory in all its manifestations and if he insists that it is "neither allegorical nor topical," how can it be Catholic? If there is no literal reference to Christ or the Church and no allegorical level of meaning, the work cannot be Catholic. It's as simple as that. And yet it can't be as simple as that because Tolkien also insists that it is "religious and Catholic," prefixing the assertion with "of course," as if to state that the religious and Catholic dimension is obvious.

The mystery deepens when we realize that Tolkien refers to *The Lord of the Rings* on another occasion as being an allegory. Replying to a letter in which he was asked whether *The Lord of the Rings* was an allegory of atomic power, he replied that it was "not an allegory of Atomic power, but of *Power* (exerted for Domination)." Having confessed the allegory of power, he asserted that this was not the most important allegory in the story: "I do not think that even Power or Domination is the real center of my story. . . . The real theme for me is about something much more permanent and difficult: Death and Immortality."[3]

It seems, therefore, that Tolkien contradicts himself, describing his work as an allegory in one place and denying that it is an allegory in another. Is he confused, or is he simply guilty of employing the same word to denote two different things? Is *The Lord of the Rings* an allegory in one sense of the word and not an allegory in another?

Clearly Tolkien is not confused about the meaning of allegory. He was a philologist and professor of language and literature at Oxford University. As such, we can safely assume that he is using the word *allegory* in two distinct senses. In one sense, *The Lord of the Rings* is an allegory; in another sense, it is not.

Perhaps, at this juncture, it would be helpful if we took a moment to discuss the various meanings of *allegory*. Linguistically, *allegory* derives from the Greek word *allegoria*, itself a combination of two Greek words: *allos*, meaning "other," and *agoria*, meaning "speaking." At its most basic level, therefore, an allegory is anything that speaks of another thing. In this sense, every word we use is an allegory. A word is a label that signifies a thing. A word, if spoken, is a noise that points our mind's eye to the thing the noise signifies; if written, it is a series of shapes that point our mind's eye to the thing the series of shapes signify. It is indeed astonishing to realize that we cannot even think a single thought without the use of allegory, a mysterious fact that subjects all perceptions of reality to the level of metaphysics, whereby the literalness of matter is always transcended by the allegory of meaning.

It is clear that Tolkien could not have had this basic meaning of allegory in mind. At this level of understanding, *The Lord of the Rings* is obviously an allegory because it couldn't possibly be anything else. This being so, let's continue with our exploration of the different types of allegory so that we can discover what sort of allegory *The Lord of the Rings* is and what sort of allegory it isn't.

The most elevated form of allegory, or at least the most sanctified, is the parable. This is the form adopted by Christ to convey the truth He wished to teach. The prodigal son did not exist in reality; he was a figment of Christ's imagination. Yet the story of the prodigal son has a timeless applicability because we can all see something of ourselves and others in the actions of the protagonist and perhaps also in the actions of the forgiving father and the envious brother. Insofar as the parable reminds us of ourselves or others, it is an allegory. Insofar as Frodo or Sam or Boromir remind us of ourselves or others, *The Lord of the Rings* is an allegory.

A far less subtle type of allegory is the formal, or crude, allegory, in which the characters are not persons but personified abstractions. They do not have personalities but merely exist as cardboard cutouts signifying an idea. For instance, Lady Philosophy in Boethius's *The Consolation of Philosophy* is not a person but a personified abstraction. She exists purely and simply to signify the beauty and wisdom of philosophy. Similarly, the character Christian in John Bunyan's *The Pilgrim's Progress* is not a person but a personified abstraction who exists purely and simply to signify the Christian believer on his journey from worldliness to otherworldliness. As a formal allegory, every character in Bunyan's story is a personified abstraction. C. S. Lewis echoes Bunyan's method in *The Pilgrim's Regress* by introducing characters such as a beautiful maiden in shining armor called Reason who has two beautiful younger sisters called Theology and Philosophy.

Tolkien is evidently referring to this kind of allegory in the foreword to the second edition of *The Lord of the Rings*. He cordially disliked such allegories because they enslaved the imaginative freedom of the reader to the didactic intentions

of the author. In order to teach and preach, the author of a formal, or crude, allegory dominates the reader's imagination, forcing the reader to see his point. Whereas good stories bring people to goodness and truth through the power of beauty, formal allegories shackle the beautiful so that goodness and truth become inescapable. Such allegories may have the good and noble purpose of teaching or preaching, but they do so at the expense of the power and glory of the imaginative and creative relationship between a good author and his readers.

It goes without saying that *The Lord of the Rings* is not this sort of allegory.

Many other forms of allegory could be discussed, such as the intertextuality employed most memorably by T. S. Eliot in "The Waste Land" or the way allegory is subsumed with great subtlety and dexterity within the works of Homer and Shakespeare and by modern novelists such as Evelyn Waugh. Although there is no obvious employment of intertextuality in Tolkien's work (though it is present), there are numerous parallels between the ways allegory is subsumed in *The Lord of the Rings* and the manner in which this is achieved by the greatest writers of epics, tragedies, comedies, and novels. It's not possible within the constraints of the present volume to discuss and analyze these fascinating parallels, but the discerning reader will detect the similarities in approach as we illustrate and illumine Tolkien's technique in the following chapters.

There is, however, one literary form of allegory that must be discussed if we are to truly understand how *The Lord of the Rings* can be seen, as its author described it, as "a fundamentally religious and Catholic work." This literary form is the fairy story, of which Tolkien's story is perhaps the greatest ever told.

One of the greatest proponents and exponents of the power and truth to be found in fairy stories is G. K. Chesterton, a writer who exerted a profound influence on Tolkien. In the chapter "The Ethics of Elfland" in his book *Orthodoxy*, Chesterton wrote persuasively and with great eloquence in defense of fairy stories:

> My first and last philosophy, that which I believe in with unbroken certainty, I learnt in the nursery. . . . The things I believed most then, the things I believe most now, are the things called fairy tales. They seem to me to be the entirely reasonable things. They are not fantasies: compared with them other things are fantastic. . . . Fairyland is nothing but the sunny country of common sense. It is not earth that judges heaven, but heaven that judges earth; so for me at least it was not earth that criticized elfland, but elfland that criticized the earth.[4]

For Chesterton and Tolkien, the goodness, truth, and beauty of fairy stories are to be found in the way they judge the way things are from the perspective of the way things ought to be. The *should* judges the *is*. This is the way things ought to be. We do not condone selfishness merely because it is normal, nor should we. A healthy perspective always judges selfishness—most especially our own selfishness—from the perspective of selflessness. In the language of religion, we always judge sin from the perspective of virtue, that which is wrong from the perspective of that which is right. Fairy stories share with religion the belief in objective morality, which is the fruit of the knowledge of the union of the natural with the supernatural and therefore the communion of the one with the other. This moral perspective is condemned by the materialist and the relativist, which is why such people are equally skeptical of the respective value of fairy stories and religion, seeing both as intrinsically untrue.

Chesterton countered the dogma of the materialist that there was nothing but matter by insisting that materialism had imprisoned the spirit of man within the three-dimensioned walls of space. Materialists emphasized the "expansion and largeness" of the cosmos and "popularized the contemptible notion that the size of the solar system ought to over-awe the spiritual dogma of man." The materialist, Chesterton wrote, was imprisoned and "seemed to think it singularly inspiring to keep on saying that the prison was very large."

> It was like telling a prisoner in Reading gaol that he would be glad to hear that the gaol now covered half the county. The warder would have nothing to show the man except more and more large corridors of stone lit by ghastly lights and empty of all that is human. So these expanders of the universe had nothing to show us except more and more infinite corridors of space lit by ghastly suns and empty of all that is divine.[5]

One is reminded in this context of Oscar Wilde, himself at one time a prisoner in the real-life Reading Gaol, who remarked that "we are all in the gutter but some of us are looking at the stars."[6] For the materialist, such as

Eustace in *The Voyage of the Dawn Treader* (until he learns better), a star is nothing but "a huge ball of flaming gas,"[7] barely worth looking at except from the perspective of a purely scientific curiosity. For such materialists, who refuse to believe in anything but the "huge ball of flaming gas," the sun is mere matter and therefore of the same "stuff" as the gutter. For these materialists, who spurn fairy stories as a mere flight from reality, there is nothing other than the gutter and therefore little point in looking beyond it. Realism, for the materialist, is the gutter itself. Realistic literature should, therefore, keep its eyes firmly fixed on the gutter and away from any unrealistic flights of fancy in the direction of the stars. In contrast to these self-proclaimed "realists," lovers and tellers of fairy stories, such as Wilde, Chesterton, Lewis, and Tolkien, see the stars as signifying a higher reality beyond the gutter. For these lovers of fairy stories, the star is not merely a ball of flaming gas but also an allegory, a thing of beauty signifying a beauty beyond itself and light in the darkness pointing to the light beyond all darkness. It is for this reason that Samwise Gamgee proclaims in one of the darkest moments in *The Lord of the Rings* that "above all shadows rides the sun."[8] For hobbits and elves, and those who see with the eyes of hobbits and elves, the sun is a signifier of the giver of all light who vanquishes all shadows.

In his seminal essay "On Fairy Stories," Tolkien takes up the Chestertonian view of fairytales against the myopic view of the materialist, enabling us to see fairytales as he sees them and—implicitly and by extension—enabling us to see his own epic fairy story, *The Lord of the Rings*, as he sees it.

Answering the charge that fairytales are escapist, Tolkien readily concedes that escape is one of their main functions: "Why should a man be scorned, if, finding himself in prison, he tries to get out and go home? Or if, when he cannot do so, he thinks and talks about other topics than jailers and prison walls?"[9] Such escape is not merely the flight of fancy of those seeking some respite from the sufferings and miseries of life but also a laudable attempt to break through the walls of materialism that the modern philosopher has constructed around the mind of man. For a Christian—and let's not forget that Tolkien was a lifelong practicing Catholic—the world is a prison. In the words of the *Salve Regina*, one of the most popular Catholic prayers, the world is "a vale of tears" and its inhabitants, the "poor banished children of Eve," are exiles awaiting their true home in heaven. For the Christian, the world is a valley of death, a land of shadows, or the shadowlands. The light that vanquishes the shadows is not of this world but has its source in our true home beyond it. One of the purposes of fairy stories is, therefore, to enable us to evade the shadows and catch a fleeting glimpse of the beauty and freedom that awaits us beyond the prison walls.

Such "escapism" was an aspect of what Tolkien referred to as the "mystical" face of fairy stories, which points toward the supernatural.[10] This mystical dimension is important because man is not merely a creature of nature but also a supernatural creature. Because "there is a part of man which is not 'Nature,'" Tolkien wrote, there is a part of him that is "wholly unsatisfied by it."[11] One of the functions of fairy stories is to satisfy the desire of man for something beyond nature—something mystical, spiritual, and supernatural.

Another face of fairy stories is "the Mirror of scorn and pity towards Man." The fairy story, Tolkien wrote, "may be used as a *Mirour de l'Omme*," as something that shows us ourselves.[12] It is this aspect of fairy stories, a major feature of Tolkien's own fairy story, that displays most obviously and potently the allegorical dimension. In reading *The Lord of the Rings*, we are seeing a mirror of man; we are seeing ourselves, our neighbors, and the world in which we live reflected back to us in charming and sometimes alarming ways. And *The Lord of the Rings* is not only a natural mirror made of mere matter but also a magical mirror that does not permit us to see ourselves in a purely passive or detached sense. The magic of the mirror is that it has the power to change the person who looks into it. The person reading *The Lord of the Rings* will see himself and the world in a new and transfigured light. If he allows the magic to work, he will be transformed from the person he thought he was into the person he is really meant to be. It is in this sense, as the following pages will endeavor to show, that *The Lord of the Rings* is the "fundamentally religious and Catholic work" that Tolkien described it as being.

CHAPTER 2

THE MIRROR OF MAN

Apart from Tolkien's confession that *The Lord of the Rings* is "a fundamentally religious and Catholic work," he also discussed what he called a "scale of significance" concerning the "relationship between personal facts and an author's works." In his own case, he discussed "insignificant," "more significant," and "really significant" facts relating to his role as the author of *The Lord of the Rings*. He placed at the very top of this scale the fact that he was "a Christian (which can be deduced from my stories), and in fact a Roman Catholic."[1] Concerning the specifically Catholic dimension, he cited with apparent approval a critic who had seen the invocations to Elbereth and the characterization of Galadriel as "clearly related to Catholic devotion to Mary." He also referred to another critic who had seen *lembas*, the Elvish waybread, as signifying *viaticum* and the Eucharist. Commenting on the astuteness of these critics, Tolkien conceded that "far greater things may color the mind in dealing with the lesser things of a fairy-story."[2]

In the same letter, immediately after the discussion of the paramount importance of his own Christianity in the "scale of significance," Tolkien described himself as being a hobbit, thereby establishing an applicable link between the diminutive heroes in his epic and the world and people beyond the epic:

> I am in fact a *Hobbit* (in all but size). I like gardens, trees and unmechanized farmlands; I smoke a pipe, and like good plain food (unrefrigerated) . . . I like, and even dare to wear in these dull days, ornamental waistcoats. I am fond of mushrooms (out of a field); have a very simple sense of humor (which even my appreciative critics find tiresome); I go to bed late and get up late (when possible). I do not travel much.[3]

In comparing himself to a hobbit, Tolkien is establishing the applicable connection between hobbits and humanity, indicating how his own fairy story, like all good fairy stories, holds up a mirror to man, showing us ourselves. It is, however, important to know what sort of man is being shown to us in *The Lord of the Rings*. It might be good, therefore, to ask ourselves the following key and fundamental question: Who is man?

For Tolkien, a deeply committed Christian, man is not simply *homo sapiens*, a label for humanity that was only invented in the early nineteenth century and has since become synonymous with what might be termed "Darwinian man"—man as simply a "naked ape," the most intelligent of the primates. Countering such a view, Christianity sees man as a creature made in the image of God in a manner that distinguishes him radically from the rest of the animals. To reiterate Tolkien's words, "[T]here is a part of man which is not 'Nature'" and is, therefore, "wholly unsatisfied by it."[4] A better name for man is that given to him by the Greeks. The Greeks called man *anthropos*, which means "he who turns upward." Unlike the other animals, which are governed by instinct and unable to do so, man looks up at the heavens, seeking a purpose and meaning beyond the mere creature comforts of everyday life. Reiterating Wilde's epigram that we're all in the gutter, but some of us are looking at the stars, we might see the gutter as the symbol of natural instinct and the stars as the symbol of supernatural desire. Man looks up; the lesser creatures do not. Man gazes; the animal grazes.

What we see reflected back to us in the magic mirror of Middle-earth is not *homo sapiens*, who is ultimately as enslaved by instinct as are the rest of the animals, but *anthropos*, who seeks his solace in the sun and the stars, the signifiers of the light of grace, echoing the words of Samwise Gamgee that "above all shadows rides the sun."

Another understanding of man reflected back to us from Middle-earth is *homo viator*, the traveling man, the man on the journey of life, the man whose purpose is to get home by taking the adventure life throws at him. The archetypal *homo viator* in Western culture is perhaps Odysseus, but in Christian terms, the archetype is the medieval Everyman, who gets to heaven through his good works and the help of the Christian sacraments. For the Christian, every man is *homo viator*, whose sole purpose (and soul's purpose) is to travel through the adventure of life with the

goal of getting to heaven, his ultimate and only true home, facing many perils and temptations along the way.

The enemy of *homo viator* is *homo superbus* (proud man), who refuses the self-sacrifice that the adventure of life demands and seeks to build a home for himself within his "self." Such a man becomes addicted to the sins that bind him, shriveling and shrinking to the pathetic size of his gollumized self. The drama of life revolves around this battle within each of us, between the *homo viator* we are called to be, and the *homo superbus* we are tempted to become. This drama is mirrored in Middle-earth in the struggles between selflessness and selfishness within the hearts of hobbits and men.

CHAPTER 3

MIDDLE-EARTH
AND THE MIDDLE AGES

Any effort to discover the hidden meaning of *The Lord of the Rings* would be deficient and defective unless due attention is paid to Tolkien's love of Old England, Old English, and Anglo-Saxons and their language, which was evident at a meeting organized by the Catholic chaplaincy at Oxford University in the 1930s, which Tolkien attended. The speaker, Hilaire Belloc, had been invited by the university chaplain, Monsignor Ronald Knox. The event was recalled by the celebrated Jesuit Father Martin D'Arcy in his memoirs:

> In his talk Belloc came out with one of his pet themes: that the Anglo-Saxons were utterly unimportant in the history of England. Now, there was present on this occasion a man who was probably the greatest authority in the world on Anglo-Saxon subjects and was the professor of Anglo-Saxon history *[sic]* at the time. He is presently professor of English Literature at Oxford. The man's name is Tolkien, and he was a very good Catholic. . . .

Well, Tolkien disagreed profoundly with Belloc on the question of the Anglo-Saxons. He was sitting just in front of me, and I saw him writhing as Belloc came out with some of his more extreme remarks. So during the interval, I said to him, "Oh, Tolkien, now you've got your chance. You'd better tackle him." He looked at me and said, "Gracious me! Do you think I would tackle Belloc unless I had my whole case very carefully prepared?" He knew Belloc would always pull some fact out of his sleeve which would disconcert you! Now, that was a tremendous tribute from probably the greatest authority in the world at the time on that particular subject.[1]

Although Belloc and Tolkien had much in common, not the least of which was their shared and impassioned Catholicism, it is intriguing that they should differ so profoundly on the importance of the Anglo-Saxons. Belloc's view of history, for the most part astute and penetrative, was always skewed by a less than balanced Francophilia and an almost shrill Germanophobia. This was evident in his dismissive disregard of the contributions to Christian culture made by the Germanic tribes in England prior to the Norman Conquest, and his lauding of the conquest itself as having brought England into the fullness of Christendom, which was always, for Belloc, synonymous with the influence of France. In contrast, Tolkien considered Anglo-Saxon England to have been idyllically Christian. Had he had his "whole case very carefully prepared" to counter Belloc's attack on the Anglo-Saxons, he might have shown that Anglo-Saxon England was profoundly Catholic to such a degree that the saintly Englishman Boniface helped evangelize Pagan Europe, while his contemporary, the truly venerable Bede, exhibited the high culture Saxon England enjoyed in abundance. While the former converted the Germans to Christ, the latter excelled in Latin and Greek; classical and patristic literature; and Hebrew, medicine, and astronomy. Bede also wrote homilies, lives of saints, hymns, epigrams, works on chronology and grammar, commentaries on the Old and New Testament, and most famously, his seminal *Historia Ecclesiastica Gentis Anglorum*, which was translated into Anglo-Saxon by King Alfred the Great. At the time of his death in 735, Bede had just finished translating the Gospel of St. John into Anglo-Saxon. Almost six hundred years later, Dante expressed his own admiration for Bede's achievement by placing him in the *Paradiso* of his *Divina Commedia*. In addition, had Tolkien decided to accept the gauntlet that Belloc had thrown down, he might have added a host of other Anglo-Saxon saints, from St. Edmund to St. Edward the Confessor. *Pace* Belloc, Tolkien could have shown that Anglo-Saxon England was a beacon of Christian enlightenment.

It is noteworthy that Father D'Arcy, in his account of this encounter, described Tolkien as "probably the greatest authority in the world on Anglo-Saxon subjects."[2] This might indeed have been the case and is especially so in relation to the Anglo-Saxon epic *Beowulf*, arguably the single most important literary influence on *The Lord of the Rings* and a work that helps us understand the way Tolkien both conceals and reveals the deepest meaning in his own work.

Probably dating from the early eighth century, making it contemporaneous with the lives of Saints Boniface and

Bede, *Beowulf* is a wonderful and wonder-filled narrative animated by the rich Christian spirit of the culture from which it sprang, brimming over with allegorical potency and evangelical zeal. It also conveys a deep awareness of classical antiquity, drawing deep inspirational draughts from Virgil's *Aeneid*, highlighting the Saxon poet's awareness of his place within an unbroken cultural continuum.

Tolkien translated *Beowulf*, though his translation would not be published until 2014. He also wrote a scholarly essay on the epic, "The Monsters and the Critics," which is considered by many to be the most masterful critique of the poem ever written. Clearly Tolkien knew *Beowulf* well, perhaps better than anyone else of his generation, and there is no denying its seminal and definitive influence on his own work. The most obvious and inescapable parallels are those between the dragon episode in *Beowulf* and the similar episode in *The Hobbit*. The Anglo-Saxon epic, however, left its inspirational fingerprints on *The Lord of the Rings* in a more subtle way.

Beowulf is divided into three sections in which the eponymous hero fights three different monsters. In the first two sections, as Beowulf confronts and ultimately defeats Grendel and then Grendel's mother, the work is primarily a narrative in which the theological dimension is subsumed parabolically, especially in the recurring motif that human will and strength is insufficient, in the absence of divine assistance, to defeat the power of evil. This is presumably an orthodox riposte to the heresy of Pelagianism,[3] which plagued Saxon England and is a major preoccupation of Bede in his *Ecclesiastical History*, probably written around the same time as *Beowulf*.[4] *The Lord of the Rings* adopts a very similar approach in the way it subsumes the presence of grace within the fabric of the story unobtrusively and yet inescapably, something we shall turn our attention to presently. It is, however, the allegorical technique the *Beowulf* poet employs in the final section of the epic that most illumines the technique Tolkien will employ in his own epic, emulating the anonymous poet who possibly taught him more than anyone else about the art of storytelling.

The dragon section of *Beowulf* commences with the theft of "a gem-studded goblet"[5] from the dragon's hoard, an act that gains the thief nothing but provokes the destructive wrath of the dragon. Beowulf takes eleven comrades with him as he goes to meet the dragon in combat, plus the thief, "the one who had started all this strife" and who "was now added as a thirteenth to their number." Unlike the eleven who had accompanied their lord willingly, the thief was "press-ganged and compelled" to go with them, acting as their unwilling guide to the dragon's den. Clearly the *Beowulf* poet is employing numerical signification to draw parallels between Beowulf's fight to the death with the dragon (an iconic signification of the Devil) and Christ's own fight to the death with the power of evil in His Passion. Equally clearly, *Beowulf* is not a formal, or crude, allegory because no character in the epic is merely a personified abstraction. Beowulf is not literally Christ, though he could be called a figure of Christ, one who is meant to remind us of Christ; the dragon is not literally Satan, though he or it is clearly intended to remind us of the Devil. Similarly, the thief is not Judas (nor Adam) but is intended to remind us of the disciple whose act of treachery brought about his lord's death,

and the other eleven are, of course, reminiscent of the other
eleven apostles. The numerical "coincidence by design"
exhibits the poet's intention of drawing parallels between his
own story and its biblical parallel without ever succumbing
to the level of formal, or crude, allegory. Beowulf is always
Beowulf, even though he is meant to remind us of Christ.

Continuing the allusive parallels, this time with Christ's
Agony in the Garden, we are told that, on the eve of battle,
Beowulf is "sad at heart, unsettled yet ready, sensing his
death." Later, as battle is about to commence, Beowulf's
appointed followers, "that hand-picked troop," "broke
ranks and ran for their lives"—all except one, Wiglaf, who
emerges as the signifier of St. John, the only one of Christ's
apostles who remained at His side during the Crucifixion. Wiglaf reprimands his comrades for their cowardice
in deserting their lord, reminding them that Beowulf had
"picked us out from the army deliberately, honored us
and judged us fit for this action."

Prior to his death, Beowulf instructs Wiglaf to order his
men to build a burial mound in remembrance of him. After
his death, ten shamefaced warriors emerge from the woods,
indicating that the thief was not among them. At the epic's
conclusion, there are once again twelve warriors riding cer-
emoniously around the burial mound, which had been duly
constructed in accordance with Beowulf's command, indicating that the traitor had been replaced by a new member,
reminiscent of the appointment of St. Matthias to replace
Judas as the twelfth apostle.

Although nobody would suggest that *Beowulf* is an allegory in the formal, or crude, sense, it is clear that the poet

intends his audience to see suggestive parallels between Beowulf's sacrifice of himself in the battle against evil and the archetypal sacrifice of God on Calvary. For the Christian, and the *Beowulf* poet was indubitably Christian, all acts of genuine love involve the laying down of our lives for another. Furthermore, all those who genuinely love in this way are ipso facto figures of Christ, from whom all genuine love flows and toward whom all genuine love points. In true life as in true literature, all those who live and love like Christ are Christlike and can be said to be figures of Christ. Christ is the archetype of which all virtuous men, in fact and in fiction, are types. The *Beowulf* poet shows this through the use of numerical clues. Tolkien does something very similar in his work, emulating the work of his Anglo-Saxon mentor.

Tolkien supplies a clue to the deepest meaning of *The Lord of the Rings* with regard to the specific date of the destruction of the Ring. The Ring is destroyed on March 25, the most significant and important date on the Christian calendar. This is the feast of the Annunciation, the date the Word is made flesh, when God becomes man. It is also the historic date of the Crucifixion, a fact that is all too often forgotten by modern Christians because Good Friday is celebrated as a moveable feast that falls on a different date each year. This is what the *Catholic Encyclopedia* says about the significance of March 25:

> All Christian antiquity . . . recognized the 25th of March as the actual day of Our Lord's death. The opinion that the Incarnation also took place on that date is found in the pseudo-Cyprianic work *De Pascha Computus*, c. 240.

It argues that the coming of Our Lord and His death must have coincided with the creation and fall of Adam. And since the world was created in spring, the Savior was also conceived and died shortly after the equinox of spring. Similar fanciful calculations are found in the early and later Middle Ages. . . . Consequently the ancient martyrologies assign to the 25th of March the creation of Adam and the crucifixion of Our Lord; also, the fall of Lucifer, the passing of Israel through the Red Sea and the immolation of Isaac.

Let's recall at this juncture that Tolkien is both a Catholic and an eminent medievalist. He would have known of the symbolic significance of March 25, and his ascribing of this particular date as the day the Ring is destroyed has palpable and indeed seismic consequences with regard to the deepest moral and theological meanings of *The Lord of the Rings*.

Chaucer's "Nun's Priest's Tale" is another great medieval work of literature that employs the same allegorical use of significant dates Tolkien employs to convey deep moral and theological meaning. In this parable about the fall of man and his subsequent redemption by Christ on the Cross (masquerading as a fable about a rooster), we are told that the story takes place thirty-two days after the beginning of March, "the month in which the world began . . . when God first made man."[6] Apart from Chaucer's reference to the theological significance of March, he signals that Chauntecleer's "Fall" (Adam's) and the Fox's (Satan's) happen on April 1 (i.e., April Fool's Day).

In following his medieval mentors in their employment and deployment of allegorical clues to deepen the theological dimension of their stories, Tolkien infuses the genius of Christendom and its literary giants into his own timeless epic. In doing so, he is thereby situating his own work firmly within that tradition. He is also deploying those same clues to signify that *The Lord of the Rings* works its magic most profoundly on the level of theology. Because Original Sin and the One Ring are both destroyed on the same theologically charged date, they become inextricably interwoven so that the Ring is symbolically synonymous with Sin itself. Original Sin is, after all, the One Sin to rule them all and in the darkness bind them. The One Sin and the One Ring are consequently melded together by Tolkien by the shared date of their destruction. We can therefore see that, with this Ring, Tolkien weds his own work morally and theologically to the deepest truths of Christianity, forging it in the flames of his lifelong and living faith.

CHAPTER 4

THE DARKENING OF THE RING

"It is mine, I tell you. My own. My Precious. Yes, my Precious."

The wizard's face remained grave and attentive, and only a flicker in his deep eyes showed that he was startled and indeed alarmed. "It has been called that before," he said, "but not by you."

"But I say it now. And why not? Even if Gollum said the same once. It's not his now, but mine. And I shall keep it, I say."

Gandalf stood up. He spoke sternly. "You will be a fool if you do, Bilbo," he said. "You make that clearer with every word you say. It has got far too much hold on you. Let it go! And then you can go yourself, and be free."[1]

Gandalf's face, "startled and indeed alarmed," seems to reflect the face of the reader as we begin to sense that something terrible has happened since the happy ending of *The Hobbit*. In the earlier book, the power of sin manifested itself in the dragon sickness and in the darkness

that descended upon Thorin Oakenshield, the Sackville-
Bagginses, the Master of Lake-Town, and, indeed, Bilbo
himself. The Ring was, however, a relatively harmless and
seemingly benign presence. Indeed, it was a priceless tool,
the magic of which saved Bilbo's life on more than one occasion. Without its power, the might of Smaug could hardly
have been overcome. After reading *The Hobbit*, we might,
in our heart of hearts, wish for such a wonderful thing as
Bilbo's magic ring.

And yet now, in the sequel, the Ring has taken on some
terrible and alarming power that seems to have possessed
the hobbit with its demonic presence. What horrific thing
has happened to Bilbo and his precious Ring?

Well might we and the wizard be startled and alarmed.

We should, however, have guessed that something was
afoot as soon as we'd read the ominous fanfare with which
Tolkien raises the curtain on the new, darker epic:

> One Ring to rule them all, One Ring to find them,
>
> One Ring to bring them all and in the darkness bind them
>
> In the Land of Mordor where the Shadows lie.

At first, even Gandalf seems uncertain of the true nature
of the Ring and the power it possesses. It is only when
he returns to the Shire some time later that he is able to
divulge the dark and deadly secret. He tells Frodo that the
Ring is far more powerful than he'd ever dared to think, "so
powerful that in the end it would utterly overcome anyone
of mortal race who possessed it. It would possess him."[2] Now
the Ring's demonic power is truly and terrifyingly revealed.
We discover that those who possess it are possessed by it.

On one level, the Ring has now taken on the function of the dragon sickness in *The Hobbit*. If we become too attached to our possessions we will become possessed by them, or, as Christ tells us, where our treasure is, there our heart will be also.[3]

Gandalf reveals to the increasingly frightened hobbit that wearing the Ring not only is perilous but also leads to a fate that is quite literally worse than death. The one who uses the Ring to make himself invisible begins to fade until, eventually, if he uses it habitually, he disappears permanently, being doomed to walk forever "in the twilight under the eye of the Dark Power that rules the Rings."[4] Recalling Tolkien's signification of the Ring as synonymous with sin, it can be seen that the act of using the Ring is synonymous with the act of sinning. Putting the Ring on is putting sin on. The effect of sin is to cause the sinner to fade from the good world of light and love that God has made, becoming invisible in this world while becoming more visible to "the eye of the Dark Power" that rules the sins and ultimately the sinner. As Gandalf will tell Frodo after the hobbit is almost killed by the Ringwraiths while wearing the Ring, "[Y]ou were in gravest peril while you wore the Ring, for then you were half in the wraith-world yourself, and they might have seized you. You could see them, and they could see you."[5] The one who becomes addicted to the power of the Ring (sin) will ultimately exile himself from the world of light and life, condemning himself to permanent invisibility in the land of shadow.

CHAPTER 5

WHO MEANT FRODO TO HAVE THE RING?

[T]his world of ours has some purpose; and if there is a purpose, there is a person. I have always felt life first as a story: and if there is a story there is a story-teller.

—G. K. Chesterton[1]

[T]here was something else at work, beyond any design of the Ring-maker. I can put it no plainer than by saying that Bilbo was *meant* to find the Ring, and *not* by its maker. In which case you were *meant* to have it. And that may be an encouraging thought.

—Gandalf[2]

You don't really suppose, do you, that all your adventures and escapes were managed by mere luck . . . ?

—Gandalf[3]

In revealing to Frodo the power and history of the Ring, Gandalf states that the Ring is not an inanimate object but is animated by a malicious will. It looks after itself and will betray the one who possesses it, as it betrayed Gollum. It was not that Gollum mislaid the Ring, Gandalf explains, but that the Ring slipped off treacherously. It was then that Bilbo arrived, putting his hand on the Ring, "blindly, in the dark." Gandalf describes this moment as "the strangest event in the whole history of the Ring so far."[4] "There was more than one power at work, Frodo. The Ring was trying to get back to its master."[5] The wizard recounts how the will of Sauron was at work, drawing the Ring back to himself: The Ring slipped from Isildur's hand, betraying him; it caught Déagol, who was murdered; it eluded the grasp of Gollum, whom "it had devoured." After it abandoned Gollum, it was stumbled and fumbled upon by Bilbo Baggins, "the most unlikely person imaginable." "Behind that," Gandalf tells Frodo, "there was something else at work, beyond any design of the Ring-maker. I can put it no plainer than by saying that Bilbo was *meant* to find the Ring, and *not* by its maker. In which case you also were *meant* to have it. And that may be an encouraging thought."[6]

It is grimly ironic that Gandalf's words, which are among the most important in the whole story, are usually overlooked by those who refuse to see the "fundamentally religious" aspect of Tolkien's masterpiece. It's as if this crucial passage has slipped from the minds of the critics as deftly and magically as the Ring has slipped from the fingers of Isildur and Gollum. In their blindness, willful or otherwise, the critics have betrayed Tolkien's text as surely as the Ring has betrayed its possessors.

The part of this passage that critics seem to have no problem grasping is Gandalf's exposition of the supernatural power of the Ring and the supernatural power of its demonic master. But as Gandalf asserts in no uncertain terms, there was more than one power at work. Apart from the demonic and malicious will of Sauron and its malevolent presence in the Ring, "there was something else at work, beyond any design of the Ring-maker." It is this "something else" that critics seem reluctant to see or acknowledge. This "something else" meant Bilbo to find the Ring. The fact that Gandalf lays emphasis on the word *meant* means he intends to emphasize that the "something else" means things to happen. By extension, of course, it also means that Tolkien, in choosing to have Gandalf stress this word, means us to get the point that the "something else" intends Bilbo to stumble upon the Ring in the dark. Gandalf could indeed "put it no plainer," nor could Tolkien. But as Chesterton says of those critics who invariably misread his own works of fiction, "If I make the point of a story stick out like a spike, they carefully go and impale themselves on something else."[7]

Bilbo being meant to find the Ring and Frodo being meant to have it is "an encouraging thought" because the "something else" is a benign supernatural power that has its own plans for the Ring "beyond any design of the Ring-maker." The "something else" is obviously God and that which is meant by God to happen is clearly providence. It is this scarcely concealed presence of God, made manifest in His providence, which makes *The Lord of the Rings* a "fundamentally religious" work. What makes it a specifically Catholic work is the relationship between providence and free will.

Although God meant Bilbo to find the Ring and Frodo to have it, he doesn't force either of the hobbits to behave in a way that would subjugate their freedom. The prompting of providence provides them with the opportunity to make good moral choices that will, in turn, have good moral consequences, but it doesn't force them to make those choices. They are free to choose well, as prompted by grace, or to choose poorly, as tempted by pride. It is this mystical interplay of providence and free will that supplies the specifically Catholic dynamic that drives the narrative forward. This is illustrated a few pages later in another potent and important exchange between Gandalf and Frodo.

Speaking of Gollum, Frodo says that it was "a pity that Bilbo did not stab that vile creature, when he had a chance."

"Pity?" Gandalf replies. "It was Pity that stayed his hand. Pity, and Mercy; not to strike without need. And he has been well rewarded, Frodo. Be sure that he took so little hurt from the evil, and escaped in the end, because he began his ownership of the Ring so. With Pity."[8]

Here we see the interplay of providence and free will illustrated clearly. Pity and mercy, both accentuated by Tolkien through the use of uppercase letters, are moral choices made freely by Bilbo. The positive consequence of his virtuous choice is to be "well rewarded" by the protection such virtue provides from the evil power of the Ring. The fact that the virtuous act is rewarded suggests the presence of one who rewards the virtuous with protection from evil.

Gandalf, who is clearly mystically attuned to the interplay of free will and providence, already senses prophetically that Bilbo's virtuous choice in sparing Gollum when

he could have killed him will have great providential consequences: "I have not much hope that Gollum can be cured
before he dies, but there's a chance of it. And he is bound up
with the fate of the Ring. My heart tells me that he has some
part to play yet, for good or ill, before the end; and when
that comes, the pity of Bilbo may rule the fate of many—
yours not least."[9]

CHAPTER 6

THE ENIGMA OF TOM BOMBADIL

And even in a mythical Age there must be some enigmas,
as there always are. Tom Bombadil is one (intentionally).

—J. R. R. Tolkien[1]

Those who have only seen Peter Jackson's film version
of *The Lord of the Rings* will have little or no idea who
exactly Tom Bombadil is. Yet even those who have read
the story and know Bombadil is a character—omitted by
Jackson—who appears early in the book, saving Merry and
Pippin from the clutches of Old Man Willow and later saving all four hobbits from the Barrow-wights, will have little
real idea who exactly this mysterious person is. The fact is
that Tom Bombadil is an enigma, a puzzling riddle who
continues to baffle and confuse readers and those critics
who endeavor to explain him. Tolkien describes him as an
intentional enigma. He is, therefore, meant to be a mystery.
He is nonetheless an important character who we ignore at
our peril.

Bombadil had existed in Tolkien's imagination prior to the writing of *The Hobbit* and a full two decades before the publication of *The Lord of the Rings*. He was introduced to the reading public in 1934 when Tolkien's long poem, "The Adventures of Tom Bombadil," was published in *Oxford Magazine*.

The character in the poem shares many characteristics with the Bombadil who appears in *The Lord of the Rings*. He is a merry fellow whose adventures take place in a landscape that would come to full fruition in the later epic and who crosses paths with some of the characters who reemerge in the book. Writing of this earlier Bombadil, Tolkien referred to him as "the spirit of the (vanishing) Oxford and Berkshire countryside,"[2] suggesting that he was originally conceived as a nature spirit. This simplicity is, however, entirely inadequate to encapsulate the complexity of the Bombadil who springs to multifaceted life in *The Lord of the Rings*. This later Bombadil is elusive and evasive, slipping through our cognitive grasp even as we think we have caught him. Many critics see him as one of the angelic beings Tolkien writes about in his wider legendarium, most notably in *The Silmarillion*; some have even speculated that he is God Himself.

On the few occasions that Tolkien mentions Bombadil in his letters, he is seemingly as elusive and evasive as Tom himself. Referring to him as an "allegory" (another example of Tolkien's confession of the allegorical aspect of his work), he describes Tom as "an exemplar, a particular embodying of pure (real) natural science: the spirit that desires knowledge of other things, their history and nature, *because they are 'other'* and wholly independent of the enquiring mind, a spirit coeval with the rational mind, and entirely unconcerned with 'doing' anything with the knowledge: Zoology and Botany not Cattle-breeding or Agriculture."[3] This is certainly profound, making the crucial distinction between the purity and goodness of science and the inevitable smudge of human will that imposes itself as soon as the fruits of science are applied technologically for practical purposes. To borrow from T. S. Eliot, between the potency of the science and the existence of technology falls the shadow of man and therefore the presence of evil. Yet even this astonishingly profound allegory does not really satisfy us, in the strict sense that the Latin word *satis* means "enough." Tolkien's efforts to describe or even define Tom are not enough. We hunger for more. We feel that there is more to Tom Bombadil than Tolkien is disclosing.

Thus with a healthy hunger for truth and an appropriate spirit of adventure, let's embark on the quest for Tom Bombadil, trying to pin down this most enigmatic of characters to see whether he can shed any light on the hidden meaning of Frodo's journey.

So who is Tom Bombadil? The question is actually asked in *The Lord of the Rings* itself. "Who are you, Master?" Frodo asks.

"Eldest, that's what I am," Tom replies. "Mark my words, my friends: Tom was here before the river and the trees; Tom remembers the first raindrop and the first acorn. He made paths before the Big People, and saw the little People arriving. He was here before the Kings and the graves of the Barrow-wights. When the Elves passed westwards, Tom

was here already, before the seas were bent. He knew the dark under the stars when it was fearless—before the Dark Lord came from Outside."[4]

"Eldest, that's what I am." This is quite a claim.

The first thing a discerning reader needs to do with information such as this is to test its veracity. Is Tom Bombadil honest? Can we trust him?

There can be no real doubt that Tom is both honest and honorable. There is no need to doubt his word. He is, therefore, the Eldest. He is older than the immortal elves, the rivers and the trees—he is even older than the weather itself, remembering the first ever raindrop. Is he, or He, God? Superficially, he might seem to have shades of the Divine, but his voice is too passive and detached to be an active agent. God was not only here before the rivers and the trees; He made the rivers and the trees. God does not merely remember the first raindrop; He sent it. He didn't merely make paths before the big people or merely observe the little people arriving; He made all people, big or small, elves, men, and hobbits, sending them into the world and not simply watching them arrive.

Even if not God Himself, Tom is evidently a person who commands not only respect but also reverence. He has a certain *je ne sais quoi*, a *gravitas*, which even his *levitas* accentuates.

Perhaps what is most intriguing is his declaration that he "knew the dark under the stars when it was fearless— before the Dark Lord came from Outside." Here is a clear affirmation that he is prelapsarian, that he existed before the Fall. He predates not only the arrival of the other creatures but also the arrival of evil. A Christian can hardly fail to read these lines about an age of innocence, free of sin and corruption, before the arrival of a Dark Lord from Outside, without visions of the Garden of Eden springing to mind. This is accentuated when we recall Tolkien's allegorical reading of Tom Bombadil as exemplifying the purity of *scientia* (knowledge), which is always transcendentally good and therefore untainted by evil, as distinct from the tainting of pure science that the empowerment of man through the application of technology necessitates.

If Tom's words are beguiling, so are his actions. As Tom and his wife Goldberry set the table, the hobbits are filled with wonder as they watch: "So fair was the grace of Goldberry and so merry and odd the caperings of Tom." We are told that "they seemed to weave a single dance, neither hindering the other, in and out of the room, and round about the table."[5] The very bodily movements of Tom and his wife seem unnatural (in the good sense) because they move with such balletic grace. It is as if their very physical actions are prelapsarian, unfallen, unbroken by sin. Whereas we move clumsily, Tom and Goldberry's every move is full of the grace of a flawless dance. Similarly, Tom does not speak prosaically but sings poetically in stress-timed meter in the manner of the Old English poetry that Tolkien loved. It's as though Tolkien is suggesting that Adam and Eve, before their fall into clumsiness, would have moved with the unpracticed grace of the ballet dancer, and that, before their fall into the prosaic, they would have spoken in the purest poetry. With a stroke of commensurate genius, Tolkien implies that language itself has fallen from poetry to prose as a consequence of the Fall.

The enigmatic nature of Tom Bombadil is heightened soon afterward when he puts the Ring to his eye and laughs carelessly. How could he take so lightly and flippantly the doom-laden thing that even Gandalf feared to touch? The answer is given a moment later when Tom puts the Ring on his finger and, to the astonishment of the hobbits, does not disappear. Laughing again, he tosses the Ring into the air, making it vanish with a flash before handing it back to the distressed Frodo with a smile. Frodo, "perhaps a trifle annoyed with Tom for seeming to make so light of what even Gandalf thought so perilously important," slipped the Ring on his finger. Merry turned toward him and was astonished to see that Frodo had disappeared. Pleased (ironically) that the Ring had not lost its power, Frodo, invisible to the hobbits, begins to creep quietly away from the fireside toward the door. "Hey there!" Tom cries, glancing toward Frodo "with a most seeing look in his shining eyes": "Hey! Come Frodo, there! Where be you a-going. Old Tom Bombadil's not as blind as that yet. Take off your golden ring! Your hand's more fair without it."[6]

We are astonished to realize that the Ring, which has justifiably filled everyone with terror and dread, has no power whatsoever over Tom. He has no fear of it. He laughs at it. He doesn't disappear when he puts it on, and yet it apparently disappears when he wants it to. To cap it all, he can still see the person wearing the Ring even when the wearer is invisible to everyone else. Curiouser and curiouser. What can all this mean?

The clue is in the prelapsarian nature of Tom. He is the Eldest, who was around before sin and evil entered the world from outside, but it seems that evil, after its arrival, had not affected him. Unlike everything else in the Fallen and therefore broken cosmos, Tom is neither Fallen nor broken. He is quite literally free from sin. He is not subject to it. It has no power over him.

Although Tolkien has not yet provided the textual clue that the date of the Ring's destruction provides, we are already being given distinct and definite clues that the Ring is symbolically synonymous with sin.

Leaving the house of Tom Bombadil and continuing on their journey, the hobbits are soon captured by a Barrow-wight before being rescued once again by Tom. What happens immediately after the rescue offers more tantalizing clues to the enigma that is Tom Bombadil.

The hobbits, disoriented after their capture, are wondering where their clothes are. "You won't find your clothes again," says Tom, bounding toward them "and laughing as he danced round them in the sunlight." It was as though "nothing dangerous and dreadful had happened" and the horror in the hobbits' hearts faded as soon as they looked at him and saw the merry glint in his eyes. Telling the hobbits that clothes "are but little loss," he adds that they should cast off the ragged remnants of their clothing and run naked on the grass. Such an appeal to public nudity seems odd, perhaps scandalous, and is certainly open to misunderstanding in our post-Freudian, sex-obsessed culture. So what is one to make of this latest enigmatic twist in Tom's perplexing personality? Is there something weird about him in a very unpleasant sense? Again, we needn't worry. We know from the weaving of Tolkien's tale that

Tom is not only honest and honorable but also innocent and wise. Indeed, the depth of his character is discovered in this very Chestertonian combination of wisdom and innocence. Tom encourages the hobbits to run naked in the fields not because he's guilty of perversion but because he's utterly innocent and immune to the harmful effects of concupiscence. Lust has no more power over Tom than the Ring does, and he would no doubt laugh at an erotic image as heartily, merrily, and innocently as he had laughed at the Ring itself.

But why, one wonders, does Tolkien make such a point of incorporating this odd display of public nudity within his story? Is it necessary, or is it some strange exhibitionism on the author's part? The answer is found in the recurrence of the Edenic motif that has been so prevalent in Tolkien's unfolding of the Bombadil enigma. Just as he knew "the dark under the stars when it was fearless," he knew the innocence of nudity when it was lustless. Tom is as shameless and guiltless in the face of nudity as was the prelapsarian Adam before shame and guilt entered the Garden.

The final clue that Tom and Goldberry are in some sense emblematic of the unfallen Adam and Eve is given in Tom's naming of the hobbits' ponies. The ponies had not been given any such names by Merry, to whom they belonged, "but they answered to the new names that Tom had given them for the rest of their lives." The connection once again to the book of Genesis and the power that God gave Adam to name the beasts is all too obvious: "And the Lord God having formed out of the ground all the beasts of the earth, and all the fowls of the air, brought them to Adam to see what he would call them: for whatsoever Adam called any living creature the same is its name."[7]

After all the clues are found and all the riddles answered, we can at last see, perhaps, that the naked truth about Tom Bombadil is that he reminds us that there is a power beyond that of the Ring and beyond that of the Dark Lord who made it. He is a glimpse of the innocence that is beyond the power of sin, the hope that is beyond the power of despair, and the light that is beyond the power of darkness.

CHAPTER 7

FIGHTING THE LONG DEFEAT

I do not think that even Power or Domination is the real center of my story. . . . The real theme for me is about something much more permanent and difficult: Death and Immortality.

—J. R. R. Tolkien[1]

Actually I am a Christian, and indeed a Roman Catholic, so that I do not expect "history" to be anything but a "long defeat"—though it contains (and in a legend may contain more clearly and movingly) some samples or glimpses of final victory.

—J. R. R. Tolkien[2]

Together through ages of the world we have fought the long defeat.

—Galadriel[3]

A ny quest to discover the deepest meaning of *The Lord of the Rings* must tackle the thorny subject of death and immortality, which Tolkien insisted was the "real theme" of the work, a theme that was "much more permanent and difficult" than any allegory of power within the story. This places *The Lord of the Rings* beyond the realm of mere politics and raises it onto the higher ground of philosophy and theology. At its highest level, Tolkien's epic serves as a memento mori, a reminder of death, which, in Christian terms, should always lead to a meditation on the Four Last Things: Death, Judgment, Heaven, and Hell. Readers are invited to meditate on these as soon as they open the book because the opening page confronts them with a rather unsettling definition of who they are. In the verse that sets the ominous atmosphere for all that follows, readers are told that they are defined by their mortality, by the fact that they are born and bound to die:

Three Rings for the Elven-kings under the sky,

Seven for the Dwarf-lords in their halls of stone,

Nine for Mortal Men doomed to die

Has there ever been another poem in the whole history of English verse in which man is linked to death as often in one solitary line? Four times in only eight syllables the death knell sounds: *Mortal* (death); *Men* (death); *doomed* (death); *die* (death). We are clearly meant to get the point. Indeed, the point, like a nail, is hammered home with relentless intensity. The readers stare into the mirror of man that Tolkien sets before them and see themselves reflected as a morbidly grinning skull. Seldom since Shakespeare's *Hamlet* has a writer employed the memento mori so brazenly.

Set against the mortality of man is the immortality of the elves. If man is doomed to die, the elves are doomed not

to die. It is this tension between death and immortality that provides much of the dynamic tension that weaves its way through the work. We experience it near the beginning of the story after the hobbits meet the company of wandering elves led by Gildor Inglorion of the House of Finrod. "Wonderful folk, Elves, sir!" Samwise Gamgee exclaims to Frodo. "Wonderful!" Asked by Frodo whether he still likes them now that he's had the chance to actually meet them, Sam answers that they are above his likes and dislikes. "It don't seem to matter what I think about them. They are quite different from what I expected—so old and young, and so gay and sad, as it were."[4]

Sam's first paradoxical impressions are more perceptive than perhaps he realizes. There is indeed a sense that the elves have a gaiety tempered with sorrow and an aura of centuries of youth combined with a deep wisdom born of centuries of experience. The song that the hobbits hear the elves singing when they first encounter them, the hymn of praise to Elbereth, resonates with Marian prayers and hymns. Elbereth is the "Queen beyond the Western Seas" and the "Light to us that wander here."[5] Similarly, Mary is "Queen of heaven, the ocean star" and "Guide of the wanderer here below." Gildor introduces himself and his elven companions as "exiles,"[6] reminding Catholics of the *Salve Regina*, in which the "poor banished children of Eve, mourning and weeping in this vale of tears," beseech the prayers of the Virgin that, "after this our exile," they might see "the blessed fruit of thy womb, Jesus."

We are accustomed to think of exile in spatial terms. An exile is one who is unable to return to his homeland

and is forced to live in a foreign land. Yet the exile that is common to the elves of Middle-earth and to those who pray the *Salve Regina* is not so much an exile in space as an exile in time. Elves and men are stranded in time, marooned in the temporal wasteland, and exiled from what St. Thomas Aquinas calls their "true native land."[7] It is for this reason that Tolkien and Galadriel can both talk about the "long defeat" of history. For Tolkien, as a Christian, history cannot be anything but a long defeat because man is a fallen creature in a fallen cosmos. In such a cosmos, death is woven into the very fabric of everything, from the mortality of men to the entropic death of the energy system of the cosmos itself. More importantly, on the spiritual plane, death is present in the corrosive and corrupting effect of evil, as made manifest in sin, so that history is characterized by an endless battle between virtue and vice in which vice can never be finally conquered but always returns, fungus-like, to blight the lives of men.[8] It is only through the eyes of faith that the all too rare "glimpses of final victory" can be discerned, and even then it is in the knowledge that such a victory is only possible at the end of time.

For men, the end of time comes at the end of their relatively short time on earth, at which point, following death, the final victory may be theirs. For elves, however, doomed to deathlessness, the long defeat is seemingly interminable, causing Galadriel to lament that she and her husband, "together through ages of the world . . . have fought the long defeat."[9] Earlier, Elrond recalled the many battles over many centuries that he had fought, experiencing "many defeats, and many fruitless victories."[10] Speaking of the victory of the Last Alliance, he conceded that "it did not achieve its end. . . . Sauron was diminished, but not destroyed. His Ring was lost but not unmade. The Dark Tower was broken, but its foundations were not removed; for they were made with the power of the Ring, and while it remains they will endure."[11]

The long defeat through ages of the world. . . . Many defeats and many fruitless victories.

It is surely no wonder, considering the centuries beyond number that they have fought against a seemingly indestructible evil, that the elves consider death to be a gift bestowed upon men by God, who is known to the elves as Ilúvatar (the All-Father): "But the sons of Men die indeed, and leave the world; wherefore they are called the Guests, or the Strangers. Death is their fate, the gift of Ilúvatar, which as Time wears even the Powers shall envy."[12]

It is thus that those who are cursed with deathlessness view with envy the gift of death, and thus that Tolkien, through the medium of fairy story, provokes in his readers a profound meditation on the "permanent and difficult" theme of death and immortality. Most important is the crucial difference that emerges between immortality and eternal life. The former is being imprisoned in time and space and unable ever to get home; the latter is the escape from the long defeat into either the final victory of heaven or the final defeat of hell.

CHAPTER 8

THE THREE FACES OF EVERYMAN

True-hearted Men, they will not be corrupted. We of
Minas Tirith have been staunch through long years of
trial. We do not desire the power of wizard-lords, only
strength to defend ourselves, strength in a just cause.
And behold! in our need chance brings to light the Ring
of Power. It is a gift, I say; a gift to the foes of Mordor.
It is mad not to use it, to use the power of the Enemy
against him. The fearless, the ruthless, these alone will
achieve victory. What would not a warrior do in this
hour, a great leader? What could not Aragorn do? Or if
he refuses, why not Boromir? The Ring would give me
power of Command. How I would drive the hosts of
Mordor, and all men would flock to my banner!

—Boromir[1]

But fear no more! I would not take this thing, if it lay by
the highway. Not were Minas Tirith falling in ruin and
I alone could save her, so using the weapon of the Dark

Lord for her good and my glory. No, I do not wish for such triumphs, Frodo son of Drogo.

—Faramir[2]

Where iss it, where iss it: my Precious, my Precious? It's ours, it is, and we wants it. The thieves, the thieves, the filthy little thieves. Where are they with my Precious? Curse them! We hates them.

—Gollum[3]

One of the key elements of *The Lord of the Rings* is the struggle between objective morality, what might be termed the battle between good and evil, and the alluring charm of relativism. It is encapsulated most graphically in Gandalf's account at the Council of Elrond of his encounter with Saruman.

Saruman is angered when Gandalf greets him as "Saruman the White," declaring that, on the contrary, he is "Saruman the Wise, Saruman Ring-maker, Saruman of Many Colors." As Saruman makes this boast, Gandalf notices that Saruman's robes, "which had seemed white, were not so, but were woven of all colors." As Saruman moves, his robes "shimmered and changed hue so that the eye was bewildered."

"I liked white better," Gandalf says.

"White!" Saruman sneers. "It serves as a beginning. White cloth may be dyed. The white page can be overwritten; and the white light can be broken."

"In which case it is no longer white," Gandalf replies. "And he that breaks a thing to find out what it is has left the path of wisdom."[4]

Clearly this exchange is not merely about aesthetics. It's not about individual preferences regarding the color of the clothes we like to wear. It's about the much more fundamental question of good and evil and their ultimate meaning. For Gandalf, white is the unity of all light, signifying the unity of all goodness. By contrast, black is the absence of all light, signifying evil.

Gandalf's view is that of Tolkien's own Christian moral perspective, following the teaching of St. Augustine, that evil has no substantial existence in itself (because God does not create evil things) but is merely the absence of the light of goodness. It is for this reason that Sauron is the *Dark* Lord and for this reason that the Dark Lord's domain, Mordor, means "Black Land" or "Land of Shadow" in Elvish.

In disdaining the white, Saruman is not being wise, as he thinks, but foolish, a fact Gandalf highlights when he insists that Saruman "has left the path of wisdom." For Saruman, there is no longer a clear distinction between light and darkness, between white and black, between good and evil. He believes in his pride, with Nietzsche, that it is possible to go beyond good and evil. The white will henceforth be subject to his will. He will do with it what he wants, subjecting goodness to his own pride and refusing to be subject to it. In short, he has ceased to accept the creed of moral objectivity and has embraced relativism.

Considering Tolkien's use of breaking the unity of white light into the "many colors" of the spectrum as a symbol for relativism, it is indeed ironic that today's radical relativists, in the branding and brandishing of their self-adulating and self-justifying "Pride," have adopted the rainbow as their symbol. As Oscar Wilde would no doubt remind us, art doesn't always follow life; sometimes life follows art.

Although the exchange between the two wizards serves as the most graphic depiction of the struggle between objective morality and relativism in *The Lord of the Rings*, it is present throughout the epic in the struggle that various characters have with the power of the Ring, not the least of which is Boromir's own epic struggle with its alluring influence.

In many respects, Boromir's struggle is most applicable to our own struggle with pride and its relativism because he is the character in *The Lord of the Rings* who is seemingly most meant to represent us. He is, after all, the only man in the Fellowship of the Ring. There are four hobbits, one wizard, one king, one elf, one dwarf—and one man. Because he is clearly the representative of humanity within the story itself, he is also, by applicable extension, our representative. This is a somewhat sobering realization because Boromir is the traitor who succumbs to the power of the Ring, seeking to take it by force from Frodo. Humanity, it seems, is the problem. And yet Boromir's motives are not devoid of noble intention. His homeland is about to be invaded by an "evil empire," far worse than the Soviet empire to which Ronald Reagan applied that label. Its leader is not a communist politician, like Yuri Andropov, who was the Soviet leader at the time of Reagan's "evil empire" speech in 1983, but is the Dark Lord himself, a demonic being described in *The Silmarillion* as the greatest of all Satan's servants.[5] The storm troopers of this demonically led army are not human beings (for the most part) but orcs. The invading army is so large that Boromir's homeland of Gondor has no reasonable chance of repelling the invaders, and Gondor's capital city, Minas Tirith, once besieged, is almost certain to fall. In the midst of this time of impending doom, the One Ring, the ultimate weapon of mass destruction, is put within Boromir's reach. He sees it as a gift to be seized. It would be "mad not to use it, to use the power of the Enemy against him."

Doesn't Boromir's reasoning seem reasonable enough? By any criteria, the defense of Minas Tirith against the evil forces of Mordor can be considered a just war. It's almost as if hell itself is marching on Gondor. What can be wrong with using the Ring against Sauron and his servants? What can be wrong with using the enemy's weapon against him? Might we not be as tempted as Boromir if we found ourselves in his position? Might we not justify the use of nuclear weapons or chemical weapons to defend our homeland from its evil enemies? Isn't Boromir's dilemma a little closer to home than we realized? Isn't the temptation that he faced one that we could face also?

The problem is that nothing ever justifies abandoning objective morality in favor of relativism. It is never licit to use evil means for a good end. The moment that we do so, we are no longer fighting against evil but are becoming evil. If we defeat an evil empire using evil means, we will only be replacing one evil empire with a new one. If Minas Tirith had defeated the forces of Mordor using the power of the Ring, Minas Tirith would have become evil in the process. In such a situation, as any loyal subjects of Minas Tirith would know, the city would not have won, but would have lost. Evil would have triumphed. The wise, such as Gandalf, Elrond, Aragorn, and Frodo, know this. The foolish, such as Saruman and Boromir, do not. The difference between Saruman and Boromir, however, is that Boromir sees the folly of his ways and repents whereas Saruman does not. Indeed, Boromir's repentance, as seen in his final meeting with Aragorn, as he lies dying, is one of the most moving and beautiful scenes in the whole of *The Lord of the Rings*.

It is intriguing, though perhaps not surprising, that Boromir's actions after his grave sin in attempting to take the Ring by force from Frodo reflect precisely the actions required of the penitent according to the form of the Sacrament of Confession in the Catholic Church. The Church teaches that there are three acts required by the penitent before the priest, acting *in persona Christi*, can absolve the penitent of his sins. These three acts are contrition (sorrow for the sin committed), confession of the sin to the priest, and satisfaction in terms of an act of penance being performed.

Boromir shows contrition for his sin a few moments after he has committed it. Having cursed Frodo and all hobbits "to death and darkness," he catches his foot on a stone and falls headlong to the ground, "as if his own curse had struck him down," and then, weeping, rises to his feet and begs Frodo to return, lamenting the "madness" that had overtaken him.[6] Shortly afterward, in an act of love which, in the words of Christ, there is no greater, he lays down his life for his friends, becoming mortally wounded in his efforts to defend the hobbits. After Aragorn discovers Boromir, pierced with many arrows and surrounded by dead orcs, he takes on the symbolic role of priest, *in persona Christi*, who hears the fallen warrior's confession. Boromir's words contain all three prerequisites for a good and holy confession: "I tried to take the Ring from Frodo [confession]. I am sorry [contrition]. I have paid [satisfaction]." Aragorn's reply to Boromir's final words fulfills the role of Christ, acting through the ordained ministry of the priest, in absolving the penitent of his sin. After Boromir laments his failure, Aragorn takes his hand, kisses his brow and responds with words of comfort and absolution: "No! You have conquered. Few have gained such a victory. Be at peace! Minas Tirith shall not fall!"[7]

As Boromir hears Aragorn's words, he smiles. It is his last act before he dies.

Clearly, the conquest and the victory Aragorn speaks of must be the spiritual victory over sin because, in a purely worldly sense, Boromir has indeed failed. Merry and Pippin have been taken prisoner by the orcs, Frodo and Sam have disappeared, and the Fellowship has been broken. This is not a victory in any worldly sense but rather a resounding defeat. In Christian terms, however, having made such a contrite confession of his sin and having paid by laying down his life for his friends, he has indeed conquered and won a great victory (though it requires the grace of God represented symbolically by the presence of Aragorn *in persona Christi*, serving as a figure of Christ, whose absolution "Be at peace!" confirms the conquest of evil and the victory Boromir has won).

It can be presumed that Boromir, as a deathbed penitent who has sacrificed his life in an act of love for his friends, is en route to his heavenly reward, which is presumably the victory Aragorn speaks of and the fruit of the conquest of sin. Thus it seems the person in the Fellowship of the Ring who represents us is not a Judas figure after all but more like a figure of St. Mary Magdalene, the repentant sinner who is destined to live happily ever after. Perhaps the "Mirror of scorn and pity" that Tolkien is showing us is not so bad after all.

In fact, as the story unfolds, and as another figure of man emerges in the character of Faramir, Boromir's saintly brother, it seems that the image of man that Tolkien reveals to us is almost aglow with the light of humanity's heavenly halo!

As a preamble to any discussion of Faramir, we need to clarify that we are dealing with the character that Tolkien created, not the travesty that Peter Jackson presents in his film version. Whereas Tolkien's character is both noble and holy, Jackson's is conflicted and acts in ways that the real Faramir (i.e., Tolkien's Faramir) would never have contemplated, let alone sanctioned. Enough of Jackson's vandalism. Let's return to Tolkien's epic.

Faramir's sanctity (and there is no other adequate word for it) is revealed when he tells Frodo that he would not take the Ring even if he found it lying at the side of the road: "Not were Minas Tirith falling in ruin and I alone could save her, so, using the weapon of the Dark Lord for her good and my glory. No, I do not wish for such triumphs, Frodo son of Drogo."[8] Because Faramir's words dovetail so well with the earlier words of Boromir, serving as their antidote, and since Tolkien has connected the two in our minds by making them brothers, it is clear that Faramir is being presented as Boromir's alter ego. As such, he is also a representative of humanity—Everyman's other self, so to speak. Whereas Boromir's pride had blinded him to the folly of using evil to defeat evil, Faramir's humility sees that there can never be a bona fide reason to employ evil means for an ostensibly good end. This is summed up in his earlier declaration that he "would not snare even an orc with a falsehood."[9] Faramir is so much a servant of the morally objective good that he would not tell even the smallest lie to the Devil himself.

If a good fairytale holds up "the Mirror of scorn and pity towards Man," as Tolkien insists in his essay "On Fairy Stories," one could justifiably argue, from Tolkien's presentation of man in the characters of Boromir and Faramir, that he fails to practice what he preaches. Although human weakness is shown in Boromir's prideful fall into relativism, he ends as a worthy and ultimately victorious penitent. As for Faramir, his apparently flawless virtue shows us nothing worthy of our scorn. There is, however, one other figurative representative of humanity in which we fail to recognize our own scornful and pitiful selves at our peril. That pathetic figure reflecting the readers back to themselves very uncomfortably is Gollum. Seldom or perhaps never in the field of human literature has the human soul in a state of addiction to sin been portrayed with such psychological realism and spiritual brilliance. Oscar Wilde tried something similar in *The Picture of Dorian Gray*, but the portrait of Dorian Gray's soul is dumb and speaks only through the screaming silence of its cruel and sadistic ugliness. Gollum is, however, a fully embodied image of the sin addict's soul. He brings to life with monstrous vigor the words of Christ that everyone who sins is a slave to sin[10] and the teaching of St. Paul about the slavery of sin.[11] As a mirror of scorn and pity toward man, he is so powerful that we only have to visualize Gollum as the shriveled wreck of our sin-enslaved soul to shiver in horror and disgust at the vision being presented to us. It's as though the English language needs a new verb, to gollumize, so that we can express the grim and graphic reality of this vision of the reality of sin.

It is, therefore, in the characters of Faramir, Boromir, and Gollum that Tolkien presents to us the three faces of Everyman. In Faramir we see the face of the saint (paradisal man), in Boromir we see the face of the repentant sinner (purgatorial man), and in Gollum we see the face of the unrepentant sinner, enslaved to his vice (infernal man). Putting it another way, we are being shown the saint, the sinner who is trying to be a saint, and the sinner who is trying to be a sinner. These three faces of man—along with the face of the man on the journey of life (*homo viator*), which we see in Frodo's carrying of his cross and Sam's faithful discipleship— illustrate the hall of mirrors with which, in multifarious ways, this most realistic of fantasies shows us ourselves.

CHAPTER 9

WORDS MADE FLESH

In a letter written in 1958, Tolkien discussed the significance of his "taste in languages," which was "obviously
a large ingredient in *The Lord of the Rings*."[1] In the same
letter, he quoted with evident approval a correspondent
who had seen a connection between *lembas*, the Elvish
waybread, and *viaticum*, which is the term used in the
Catholic Church for the Eucharistic host administered to
the dying. This connection is accentuated by the linguistic
link between the two words. *Viaticum* essentially means
waybread, from the Latin *via*, meaning "way," and from the
fact that the thing being given "for the way" is bread. It is
sacramental bread to nourish the soul on its journey from
this life to everlasting life.

Lembas is synonymous linguistically with *viaticum*
because in Sindarin, one of Tolkien's invented Elvish languages, it literally means "way-bread" or "journey-bread."
In Quenya, another of Tolkien's Elvish languages, *lembas*
means "life-bread" or "bread of life." Linguistically, therefore, *lembas* is identified as being both *viaticum* (way-bread)

and the Eucharistic host (bread of life), which is why Tolkien agreed with a correspondent who had seen it as "a derivation from the Eucharist."[2]

The implicitly religious aspect of *lembas* was accentuated in another letter in which Tolkien objected to the waybread being described as a "food concentrate," which he condemned as exemplifying a tendency toward "scientification" that was "alien" to his story. "No analysis in any laboratory would discover chemical properties of *lembas* that made it superior to other cakes of wheat-meal," he wrote. Its power was, therefore, not physical, in a manner that could be measured by science, but spiritual. Its "significance," Tolkien insisted, was "of what one might hesitatingly call a 'religious' kind."[3] Illustrating the point, he stated that the religious element becomes particularly apparent in the chapter of *The Lord of the Rings* entitled "Mount Doom," referring presumably to this passage: "The *lembas* had a virtue without which they would long ago have lain down to die. It did not satisfy desire, and at times Sam's mind was filled with the memories of food, and the longing for simple bread and meats. And yet this waybread of the Elves had a potency that increased as travelers relied on it alone and did not mingle it with other foods. It fed the will, and it gave strength to endure, and to master sinew and limb beyond the measure of mortal kind."[4]

A Catholic reading about this "magical" or miraculous power of the Elvish waybread might well be reminded of those saints who had apparently lived on nothing but the Eucharist for long periods. Indeed, Blessed Alexandrina da Costa seemingly lived on the Eucharist alone for many years prior to her death on October 13, 1955, a week before the final part of *The Lord of the Rings* was published. This medically impossible phenomenon, which was unfolding throughout the whole period of Tolkien's writing of *The Lord of the Rings*, was monitored by skeptical scientists who attested to its inexplicable nature. Dr. Gomez de Araujo of the Royal Academy of Medicine in Madrid, a specialist in nervous diseases and arthritis, confirmed in the official medical report of the phenomenon that it was "scientifically inexplicable. . . . It is absolutely certain that during forty days of being bedridden in hospital, the sick woman did not eat or drink and we believe such phenomenon could have happened during the past months, perhaps the past thirteen months leaving us perplexed." In addition to the formal medical report, there was a certificate signed by two other distinguished scientists that independently confirmed the report's conclusion:

> We the undersigned, Dr. C. A. di Lima, Professor of the Faculty of Medicine of Oporto and Dr. E. A. D. de Azevedo, doctor graduate of the same Faculty, testify that, having examined Alexandrina Maria da Costa, aged 39, . . . have confirmed her paralysis. . . . And we also testify that the bedridden woman, from 10 June to 20 July 1943 remained in the sector for infantile paralysis at the Hospital of Foce del Duro, under the direction of Dr. Araujo and under the day and night surveillance by impartial persons desirous of discovering the truth of her fast. Her abstinence from solids and liquids was absolute during all that time. We testify also that she retained her weight, and her temperature, breathing, blood pressure,

pulse and blood were normal while her mental faculties were constant and lucid. . . .

The examination of the blood, made three weeks after her arrival in the hospital, is attached to this certificate and from it one sees how, considering the aforesaid abstinence from solids and liquids, science naturally has no explanation. The laws of physiology and biochemistry cannot account for the survival of this sick woman for forty days of absolute fast in the hospital, more so in that she replied daily to many interrogations and sustained very many conversations, showing an excellent disposition and a perfect lucidity of spirit. As for the phenomena observed every Friday at about 3 p.m. [i.e. her ecstasies], we believe they belong to the mystical order. . . . For the sake of the truth, we have prepared this certificate which we sign. Oporto, 26 July 1943.[5]

News of this apparent miracle spread far and wide, especially in the Catholic world, and one wonders whether Tolkien was aware of it as he was writing of the miraculous powers of *lembas*. Yet even if he had not heard of the miraculous news from Portugal, he would have been aware of well-known Catholic saints, such as St. Catherine of Siena and St. Catherine of Genoa, who were reputed to have lived for long periods on nothing but the Eucharist. In any event, and practical examples notwithstanding, the powers attributed to *lembas* in the previously quoted passage accord exactly with those ascribed to the Blessed Sacrament in Eucharistic theology. We are told that *lembas* possesses "a virtue" that is life sustaining in a supernatural sense, without which Frodo and Sam "would long ago have lain down to die." It has "a potency that increased as travelers relied on it alone and did not mingle it with other foods." It feeds the will and gives strength to endure, providing mastery over the body "beyond the measure of mortal kind"— that is, above what is humanly possible. The very notion of a food feeding the will, as distinct from simply the body, places it beyond mere physical nourishment and elevates it to the metaphysical level. Virtue requires grace to nourish the will, enabling the will to overcome its weakness. *Lembas*, like the Eucharist, provides this grace. It is little wonder that Tolkien, albeit "hesitatingly," insisted that the significance of *lembas* was "religious."

In the light of Tolkien's admission or confession that *lembas* is connected to the Eucharist, it is intriguing to conjecture whether he succumbed to a punning reference to the Eucharistic connection when the Fellowship are first introduced to the Elvish waybread in Lothlórien. After Gimli mistakes *lembas* for *cram*, the waybread made by the men of Dale, he is told by the elves that *lembas* "is more strengthening than any food made by Men, and it is more pleasant than *cram*, by all accounts."

"Indeed it is," Gimli replies, comparing it favorably to the honey cakes of the Beornings, which, he adds, is "great praise, for the Beornings are the best bakers that I know of." Highly pleased, the dwarf is fulsome in his expression of gratitude, exclaiming that the elves "are kindly hosts."[6] Is it possible that the use of "hosts" in the context of the goodness of *lembas* is a deliberate pun on Tolkien's part, or, perhaps, is it the case of his unconscious or subconscious mind inserting itself surreptitiously? After all, as Tolkien

himself proclaimed, "far greater things may color the mind in dealing with the lesser things of a fairy-story."[7] Reminding ourselves of Tolkien's other confession that *The Lord of the Rings* is "a fundamentally religious and Catholic work; unconsciously so at first, but consciously in the revision," might we see this as being either a conscious revision made by the author to ensure its fundamentally religious and Catholic character or, alternatively, an unconscious pun, stealing itself into the text unnoticed as the muse moved mystically through the author's mind?

If the former, it constitutes a rather amusing joke on the author's part, a deliberate and whimsical clue embedded within the story; if the latter, the clue was left by apparent accident enabling us to say, paraphrasing Gandalf, that there was something else at work, beyond any design of the storyteller. It can be put no plainer than by saying that the reader is meant to find the pun, and not by its maker. And that is indeed an encouraging thought.

CHAPTER 10

WORDS AND WIZARDS

The fact that Tolkien had a predilection for riddles and wordplay is evident from their prominent presence in *The Hobbit*. They are also present, though less prominently, in *The Lord of the Rings*, not least when the Fellowship arrives at the Gates of Moria. Gandalf reads the inscription on the gates, which is written in the elven tongue of the Elder Days: "The Doors of Durin, Lord of Mordor. Speak, friend, and enter." The wizard, failing to see the wordplay, dismisses the inscription as being of no importance. Even when Merry asks what "speak, friend, and enter" might mean, the clue is not seen.

"That is plain enough," Gimli replies, in answer to Merry's question. "If you are a friend, speak the password, and the doors will open, and you can enter."

"Yes," says Gandalf, "these doors are probably governed by words. . . . These doors have no key. . . . [I]f they were shut, any who knew the opening word could speak it and pass in."[1]

Not knowing the password, the wizard employs all his knowledge of ancient tongues and spells in order to guess the password and command the doors to open. All is in vain. Even the wizard's unfathomable store of knowledge is insufficient. Eventually he collapses to the ground, "his head bowed, either in despair or in anxious thought." Then with a startling suddenness, he springs to his feet, laughing. "I have it!" he cries. "Of course, of course! Absurdly simple, like most riddles when you see the answer. . . . The opening word was inscribed on the archway all the time! The translation should have been: *Say 'Friend' and enter.* I had only to speak the Elvish word for *friend* and the doors opened. Quite simple. Too simple for a learned lore-master in these suspicious days. Those were happier times."[2]

Gandalf's final comments display a Chestertonian wisdom and innocence in which simplicity and happiness are melded into synonymous harmony. It is the same wisdom and innocence seen in the hearts of the hobbits and in the happiness and harmony found in the rustic simplicity of the Shire. It is, moreover, the same wisdom and innocence Christ is referring to when, having called a child to Him, He proclaims the following Good News: "Amen I say to you, unless you be converted, and become as little children, you shall not enter into the kingdom of heaven. Whosoever therefore shall humble himself as this little child, he is the greater in the kingdom of heaven."[3] Beyond the learning of lore-masters and the suspicions of the sophisticated is the simplicity of the child and the humility of those who have become like little children. Such are the "friends" to whom the gates of the kingdom of heaven, and the gates of the kingdom of Moria, are opened.

If the rediscovery of childlike simplicity was the key to the kingdom of Moria, the journey Gandalf now embarks on will mark him not simply as being childlike but as being Christlike. On the bridge of Khazad-Dûm, he will lay down his life for his friends in an act of love of which, in Christ's own words, there is no greater. Although his deadly and deathless foe, a Balrog, is clearly demonic, *The Lord of the Rings* does not reveal this explicitly. It is in Tolkien's other great mythopoeic work, *The Silmarillion*, that Balrogs are revealed definitively as being demons—that is, fallen angels. As he faces his demonic enemy, Gandalf describes himself as "a servant of the Secret Fire,"[4] a grandiose but beguilingly elusive title, which goes unexplained. Again, it is in *The Silmarillion* that the riddle is solved. The Secret Fire is nothing less than the very God-given being of the cosmos itself, the spark of God's life and light in His creation: "Therefore Ilúvatar [God, the "All-Father"] gave to their vision Being, and set it amid the Void, and the Secret Fire was sent to burn at the heart of the World; and it was called Eä."[5] The word *Eä* comes from the Elvish verb *to be*, the equivalent of the Latin *esse*, from which we derive *essential*, which means that it needs to be translated as "being" or "that which is." In another part of *The Silmarillion*, the word *Eä* emerges as the very word that God utters to bring the cosmos into being: "Therefore I say: *Eä!* Let these things Be! And I will send forth into the Void the Flame Imperishable, and it shall be at the heart of the World, and the World shall Be."[6] Parallels with the opening verses of Genesis are palpable: "In the beginning God created heaven, and earth. And the earth was void and empty, and darkness was upon the face of the deep; and the spirit of God moved over the waters. And God said: Be light made. And light was made."[7] Gandalf proclaims himself, therefore, to be a servant of the light of God, the Flame Imperishable, which is the very being of the cosmos itself. Even more explicitly, Tolkien told the American scholar Clyde S. Kilby that the Secret Fire could be likened to the Holy Spirit,[8] thereby making Gandalf a veritable and self-proclaimed servant of the Christian God. If this is so, the fire would of course be "secret" because the fullness of Christian Revelation had not yet been shown forth in time—though existing and therefore known in the eternal sphere to which Gandalf belongs—as an angelic being (another fact concealed in *The Lord of the Rings* but revealed elsewhere in Tolkien's writings).

Tolkien explained his reason for shrouding the supernatural element in secrecy in a letter to his Jesuit friend Father Robert Murray:

> I might perhaps have made more clear the later remarks in Vol. II (and Vol. III) which refer to or are made by Gandalf, but I have purposely kept all allusions to the highest matters down to mere hints, perceptible only by the most attentive, or kept them under unexplained symbolic forms. So God and the "angelic" gods, the Lords or Powers of the West, only peep through in such places as Gandalf's conversation with Frodo: "behind that there was something else at work, beyond any design of the Ringmaker's," or in Faramir's Númenórean grace at dinner.[9]

In the same letter, Tolkien stated that Gandalf "is not, of course, a human being (Man or Hobbit)." Although there were "no precise modern terms to say what he was," Tolkien described Gandalf and the other wizards as incarnate angels akin to the Greek messengers sent from the gods to men (or, we might add, the herald angels sent by God to man). "By 'incarnate,'" Tolkien continued, "I mean they were embodied in physical bodies capable of pain, and weariness, and of afflicting the spirit with physical fear, and of being 'killed', though supported by the angelic spirit they might endure long, and only show slowly the wearing of care and labor." The wizards were "those who know"—adding ominous potency to Gandalf's description of himself as the servant of the Secret Fire—emissaries from the supernatural order, "sent to Middle-earth, as the great crisis of Sauron loomed on the horizon."[10]

As incarnate beings, albeit supernatural in power, Tolkien explained that the wizards were prone to error, capable of choosing to serve good or succumbing to the temptations of evil.[11] As such, Gandalf, unlike Saruman, passes the moral test:

> For in his condition it was for him a *sacrifice* to perish on the Bridge in defense of his companions, less perhaps than for a mortal Man or Hobbit, since he had a far greater inner power than they; but also more, since it was a humbling and abnegation of himself in conformity to 'the Rules': for all he could know at that moment he was the *only* person who could direct the resistance to Sauron successfully, and all *his* mission was vain. He was handing over to the Authority that ordained the Rules, and giving up personal hope of success.[12]

It is significant that Tolkien makes a point of emphasizing the word *sacrifice* in his description of Gandalf's laying down his life for his friends. It is also significant that Gandalf's death is described as "a humbling and abnegation"; an emptying of himself in submission to the rules of Providence; and the handing of himself, his fellows, and the fate of Middle-earth into the hands of "the Authority that ordained the Rules"—that is, God himself. It is difficult to read this description of Gandalf's death without seeing parallels with Christ's submission of Himself to the will of the Father on Golgotha, transforming Gandalf into a figure of the Crucified Christ.

Considering the evident symbolic connection, shrouded or otherwise, between Gandalf's sacrifice and Christ's, and therefore between Khazad-Dûm and Golgotha, it is not surprising that some people have drawn the analogous connection between the Mines of Moria and the land of Moriah, the latter being the place Abraham prepared to sacrifice Isaac, an episode of the Old Testament that is seen traditionally by biblical theologians as prefiguring God's sacrifice of his own Son: "And he said, Take now thy son, thine only *son* Isaac, whom thou lovest, and get thee into the land of Moriah; and offer him there for a burnt offering upon one of the mountains which I will tell thee of."[13] It is intriguing, however, that Tolkien explicitly and even vehemently denied that there was any significant connection: "Internally there is no conceivable connexion between the mining of Dwarves, and the story of Abraham. I utterly repudiate any such significances and symbolisms."[14] What is one to make of such an unequivocal denial, especially in

light of other quite obvious linguistic connections Tolkien makes no effort to conceal but either implicitly or explicitly affirms? It is curious, for instance, that he speaks of there being no conceivable connection between the mining of Dwarves and the story of Abraham, which is true enough, but fails to even mention or discuss the all too conceivable connection between Gandalf's death—especially in light of his subsequent resurrection—and Christ's, the latter of which is always linked typologically with the story of Abraham and Isaac in Moriah. *Pace* Tolkien, the connection is real enough and the only issue is whether it was intentional on the part of the author or merely coincidental, or, dare one say, providential.

The connection between Gandalf and Christ is made even more apparent in the wizard's resurrection and by the manner in which his joyful return to life is reminiscent not only of Christ's resurrection but also of His transfiguration. Gandalf reappears in shining white garments, his hair as white as snow. Gimli, dazzled by the brightness of the wizard's robes, sinks to his knees, shading his eyes from the glare. As Gandalf wraps his old grey cloak around his white robes, "it seemed as if the sun had been shining, but now was hid in cloud again."[15] The significance of the resurrection is accentuated still further by Gandalf's assertion that his return marks the pivotal point in the story: "Be merry! We meet again. At the turn of the tide. The great storm is coming, but the tide has turned."[16] These lines reflect those in G. K. Chesterton's *Ballad of the White Horse*, which Tolkien knew well: "'The high tide!' King Alfred cried. / 'The high tide and the turn!'"[17] As with Alfred's turning back of the pagan tide sweeping across England, Gandalf's return marks the point at which the tide turns against Sauron's legions.

The sudden and unexpected turn in the story that Gandalf's resurrection and transfiguration represents is an example of what Tolkien called *eucatastrophe*, a word he invented, defining it as "the good catastrophe, the sudden joyous 'turn,'" which was a mark of all good fairy stories: "[T]his joy . . . is a sudden and miraculous grace; never to be counted on to recur. It does not deny the existence of *dyscatastrophe*, of sorrow and failure: the possibility of these is necessary to the joy of deliverance; it denies . . . universal final defeat and in so far is *evangelium*, giving a fleeting glimpse of Joy, Joy beyond the walls of the world, poignant as grief."[18]

Gandalf's resurrection, like the resurrection of Christ, is indeed a sudden and miraculous grace, offering a tantalizing glimpse of the joy of the good news (*evangelium*) beyond the walls of the world. It also conveys, like the resurrection of Christ, the promise of final deliverance from evil, the turning of the tide.

Tolkien wrote about the meaning of *eucatastrophe* in the light of the miraculous healing of a small boy at the Marian Shrine in Lourdes in 1927, connecting it with the sudden joyous turn of events that he was trying to achieve at certain moments in his work:

[A]t the story of the little boy (which is a fully attested *fact* of course) with its apparent sad ending and then its sudden unhoped-for happy ending, I was deeply moved and had that peculiar emotion we all have—though not often. It is quite unlike any other sensation. And all of a sudden I realized what it was: the very thing I have been trying to write about and explain . . . For it I coined the word 'eucatastrophe': the sudden turn in a story which pierces you with a joy that brings tears . . . And I was there led to the view that it produces its peculiar effect because it is a sudden glimpse of Truth.[19]

It can be seen, therefore, that good news is connected to bad news in a profoundly inextricable way. It is good because it vanquishes the bad. The Resurrection vanquishes death; miraculous healing vanquishes disease. Thus Tolkien's invented word *eucatastrophe* is not merely a good turn, which might be translated as *eustrophe*, but a "good-downturn" (*eu* = good; *cata* = down; *tropos* = turn). It describes the good that God, or the storyteller, brings out of evil; it is the good that could not have happened without the evil that preceded it. A eucatastrophe is the *felix culpa*, the blessed fault or fortunate fall, from which God brings forth unexpected blessings. Thus the catastrophe of the Fall brought forth the eucatastrophe of the Redemption, and the catastrophe of the Crucifixion brought forth the eucatastrophe of the Resurrection. It is in this light, which is nothing less than the divine light, that Gandalf's death and resurrection should be seen.

CHAPTER 11

WORMS AND LIZARDS

Having returned from the dead resplendent with renewed wisdom and sanctity, Gandalf delves into the mind and motives of Sauron, explaining to Aragorn how the Dark Lord's pride has rendered him blind to the plans of his enemies. Although Sauron knows the Ring is abroad and suspects it is with the Fellowship that set out from Rivendell, he does not yet perceive the purpose of his enemies. "He supposes that we are all going to Minas Tirith," Gandalf explains, "for that is what he would himself have done in our place." In his pride, Sauron fears that a mighty warrior will suddenly appear, wielding the Ring and using its power against him, seeking to cast him down so that the new Ringbearer can take his place as ruler of Middle-earth. "That we should wish to cast him down and have *no* one in his place is not a thought that occurs to his mind. That we should try to destroy the Ring itself has not yet entered into his darkest dream. In which no doubt you will see our good fortune and our hope."[1]

In this short discourse, Gandalf brings to the fore the self-destructive tendency of evil, illustrating how pride's prejudiced presumption darkens and obscures its ability to judge any situation objectively and clearly. Blinded by its self-centered bias from perceiving the selfless motives of those willing to lay down their lives self-sacrificially, pride is fooled by the humility that it does not possess, thereby unwittingly offering hope and good fortune to the meek of heart who do not see as it sees or act as it acts. This paradoxical weakness at the darkened heart of those who worship strength and power is encapsulated by Théoden. "Strange powers have our enemies, and strange weaknesses!" he exclaims to Gandalf. "But it has long been said: *oft evil will shall evil mar.*"[2]

"That many times is seen," Gandalf agrees, reiterating his own words of a few pages earlier: "Strange are the turns of fortune! Often does hatred hurt itself!"[3]

Nowhere is this self-destructive and self-mutilating aspect of evil depicted more graphically in *The Lord of the Rings* than in the manner in which the weight of the spiderlike Shelob's malice is shown to be self-defeating, crushing itself with its own cruel will: "She . . . heaved up the great bag of her belly high above Sam's head. . . . Now splaying her legs she drove her huge bulk down on him again. Too soon. For Sam still stood upon his feet, and dropping his own sword, with both hands he held the elven-blade point upwards, fending off that ghastly roof; and so Shelob, with the driving force of her own cruel will, with strength greater than any warrior's hand, thrust herself upon a bitter spike."[4]

Often does hatred hurt itself!

This discussion of the self-destructive quality of evil raises the broader question of the way in which Tolkien deals with the nature or supernature of evil in his epic. Considering the parallels with the opening book of Genesis, which Tolkien employs in his telling of the creation myth in *The Silmarillion*, and in his allegorical connection of the One Ring with the One Sin of Adam and Eve, we shouldn't be surprised to see similar parallels in his depiction of evil in *The Lord of the Rings*. There are, for instance, obvious parallels with Genesis in Gandalf's encounter with Wormtongue in Edoras. "Down, snake!" Gandalf commands Wormtongue. "Down on your belly!"[5] Such words resonate inescapably with God's words to Satan: "And the Lord God said unto the serpent, Because thou hast done this, thou *art* cursed above all cattle, and above every beast of the field; upon thy belly shalt thou go, and dust shalt thou eat all the days of thy life."[6] As if to ensure that the connection is made, Gandalf again refers to Wormtongue as a snake a few lines later: "See, Théoden, here is a snake!" Lest we should still fail to get the satanic connection, Wormtongue bares his teeth and "with a hissing breath" spits before the king's feet.[7] Thus having poisoned the ear of the king with his envenomed words, reminding us perhaps of the wicked King Claudius in *Hamlet*, Wormtongue spits like a snake before fleeing from the king's presence.

Wormtongue is indeed aptly named. *Worm*, having its root in the Old English *wurm* or *wyrm*, means "snake," "serpent," "dragon," or "lizard." Wormtongue's name translates, therefore, as "serpent-tongue" or "dragon-tongue." Once again, Tolkien's "taste in languages" informs his work with potent symbolic resonance, as it does in the naming of Melkor, the satanic figure in *The Silmarillion*, of whom Sauron is described as the greatest servant.

Melkor, later known as Morgoth, is Middle-earth's equivalent of Lucifer, or Satan. Tolkien describes him as the greatest of the Ainur, as Lucifer was the greatest of the archangels. Like Lucifer, Melkor is the embodiment and primeval perpetrator of the sin of pride and is intent on corrupting humanity for his own purposes. Melkor desired "to subdue to his will both Elves and Men, envying the gifts with which Ilúvatar promised to endow them; and he wished himself to have subjects and servants, and to be called Lord, and to be master over other wills."[8]

The parallels with the Old Testament become even more obvious when Tolkien describes the war between Melkor and Manwë, who is clearly cast in the role of the archangel Michael, Lucifer's nemesis. Manwë is "the brother of Melkor in the mind of Ilúvatar [i.e., God]" and was "the chief instrument of the second theme that Ilúvatar had raised up against the discord of Melkor."[9]

The link between Melkor and Lucifer is made most apparent in the linguistic connection between them. As a philologist, Tolkien employs language to synthesize his Satan with the biblical archetype. The original spelling of Melkor in the earliest drafts of the mythology is *Melko*, which means "the Mighty One"; *Melkor* literally means "He who arises in Might." Tolkien explains, "But that name he has forfeited; and the Noldor, who among the Elves suffered most from his malice, will not utter it, and they name

him Morgoth, the Dark Enemy of the World."[10] Similarly, *Lucifer*, brightest of the angels as Melkor is the mightiest, means "Light Bringer," whereas the Jews named him *Satan*, which means "enemy" in Hebrew. Linguistically, therefore, *Morgoth*, *Satan*, and *enemy* share the same meaning. They are the same word in three different languages. Morgoth and Satan clearly represent the same primal enemy of humanity. Tolkien's intention, both as a Christian and as a philologist, in identifying Melkor with Lucifer is plain enough.

In earlier drafts of the mythology that predate the publication of *The Lord of the Rings*, Melkor's role parallels that of the biblical Satan. He is the primal bringer of discord into Ilúvatar's design and he harbors a desire to have dominion in the world contrary to the will of Ilúvatar. In the later versions of the myth, the role of Melko, now known as Melkor, becomes more complex—itself a reflection of Tolkien's increasing concern with theological intricacy—yet Melko-Melkor-Morgoth remains essentially a depiction of Satan.

Taking his inspiration, perhaps, from the Book of Isaiah ("Thy pomp is brought down to the grave, and the noise of thy viols: the worm is spread under thee, and the worms cover thee. How art thou fallen from heaven, O Lucifer, son of the morning.")[11] Tolkien says of Melkor, "From splendor he fell through arrogance to contempt for all things save himself, a spirit wasteful and pitiless . . . He began with the desire of Light, but when he could not possess it for himself alone, he descended through fire and wrath into a great burning, down into Darkness."[12]

Shortly after this description of Melkor, Tolkien introduces Sauron, the dark enemy in *The Lord of the Rings*.

Sauron is described as a "spirit" and as the "greatest" of Melkor's—alias Morgoth's—servants, "But in after years he rose like a shadow of Morgoth and a ghost of his malice, and walked behind him on the same ruinous path down into the Void."[13] This brief depiction of Sauron in *The Silmarillion* reveals that the evil power in *The Lord of the Rings* is directly connected to Tolkien's Satan, rendering implausible a non-theistic interpretation of the book's deepest moral meaning.

Considering the obvious and obviously intentional linguistic parallels Tolkien employs to connect his Satan figure, Melkor, with his biblical equivalent, and with the brazen connection in the text of *The Lord of the Rings* of Wormtongue with the serpent in Genesis, it would seem equally obvious, one would think, that the name Sauron is connected linguistically with the Greek word *sauros*, meaning "lizard" and, by extension, "dragon" or "serpent." It is, therefore, odd—not to say bizarre—that Tolkien denied any linguistic connection between Sauron and *sauros* in the draft of a letter written in 1967.[14]

In *Morgoth's Ring*, volume ten of *The History of Middle-earth*, Tolkien is preoccupied with the figure of Melkor-Morgoth. "Above all," wrote Christopher Tolkien in his foreword to *Morgoth's Ring*, "the power and significance of Melkor-Morgoth . . . was enlarged to become the ground and source of the corruption of Arda."[15] Whereas Sauron's infernal power was concentrated in the One Ring, Morgoth's far greater diabolic power was dispersed into the very matter of Arda itself: "[T]he whole of Middle-earth was *Morgoth's Ring*."[16] The pride of Melkor-Morgoth had "marred" the whole of material creation just as, according to the Christian doctrine of the Fall, the pride of Lucifer-Satan had marred the very fabric of the world.

If, however, the shadow of Morgoth had fallen across the face of Middle-earth, marring it terribly, Tolkien asserts with Christian hope that the final victory would never belong to Morgoth. "Above all shadows rides the Sun," Samwise Gamgee affirms in the tower of Cirith Ungol,[17] and Tolkien uses the childlike wisdom of the hobbit to express deep theological truths. The sun is a metaphor for Ilúvatar, the All-Father, God Himself, and the shadow a metaphor for evil. The final triumph of good (i.e., God) and the ultimate defeat of evil were spelled out by Ilúvatar in the Ainulindalë at the very beginning of creation.

Referring to Melkor's introduction of disharmony into the great music of God's creation, Ilúvatar warned his enemy of the ultimate futility of his rebellion: "And thou, Melkor, shalt see that no theme may be played that hath not its uttermost source in me, nor can any alter the music in my despite. For he that attempteth this shall prove but mine instrument in the devising of things more wonderful, which he himself had not imagined."[18] Eventually even the evil will of Melkor will understand that all its evil actions have been the unwitting servant of unimaginable providence: "And thou, Melkor, wilt discover all the secret thoughts of thy mind, and wilt perceive that they are but a part of the whole and tributary to its glory."[19] Sauron is mighty, and Melkor is mightier still, but as Frodo exclaims at the crossroads, "They cannot conquer forever!"[20]

CHAPTER 12

MAGIC AND MIRACLE

In some Christian circles, one of the most controversial aspects of *The Lord of the Rings* is the presence of "magic." For some Christians, magic and sorcery are synonymous, making not only Tolkien's work but even C. S. Lewis's *Chronicles of Narnia* forbidden territory. The whole issue has been complicated by the phenomenal success of the *Harry Potter* books and by the legion of fantasy books and products that have seemingly saturated the market. There is no doubt that much modern fantasy is poisonous and pernicious, but it is a serious error to judge the work of Tolkien or Lewis in the light or darkness of the orc-oriented imitations and gollumized parodies that have followed in their wake.

In order to understand how "magic" is treated in *The Lord of the Rings* it is necessary to understand the hierarchy of creative value at the heart of Tolkien's philosophy of myth that animates all his creative work. This hierarchy is evident in Tolkien's famous lecture and essay "On Fairy-Stories," in his allegorical short story "Leaf by Niggle," and in his superb poem, "Mythopoeia." It is also to be found throughout his letters and is implicit in his work.

At the top of the hierarchy is the Creator, the source of all that is. Below the Creator is creation—that is, the things of nature made directly by the Creator *ex nihilo* (out of nothing). And below creation is subcreation—that is, those things made from the preexisting things of nature by rational beings, such as men or angels, with the creative gifts bestowed upon them by the Creator. Subcreation can itself be subdivided into those things made for the sole purpose of reflecting the goodness, truth, and beauty of reality (what might be called good art) and those things made for some practical utilitarian purpose (what might be called technology). Subcreation can also be subdivided between those things subcreated virtuously and those subcreated viciously.

An example of virtuous subcreation would be the beautiful cloaks the elves of Lothlórien bestow as gifts upon the Fellowship: "[G]rey with the hue of twilight under the trees they seemed to be; and yet if they were moved, or set in another light, they were green as shadowed leaves, or brown as fallow fields by night, dusk-silver as water under the stars."

"Are these magic cloaks?" asks Merry, beguiled by their astonishing beauty and the way their colors seemed to shimmer and change.

"I do not know what you mean by that," the leader of the elves answers. "They are fair garments, and the web is good, for it was made in this land. They are Elvish robes certainly, if that is what you mean. Leaf and branch, water and stone: they have the hue and beauty of all these things under the twilight of Lórien that we love; for we put the thought of all that we love into all that we make."[1]

The beauty of those things subcreated by the elves is so marvelous to the eyes of those who do not possess their subcreative gifts that there appears to be a magic in them. And yet, as the leader of the elves makes clear, their beauty is simply a reflection of the beauty of nature transfigured by the love with which the elves make things from it. Elves possess gifts of subcreation that are superior to those possessed by men or hobbits but the gift is nonetheless natural to them and therefore not magical.

Compare this natural gift of elves with the natural gifts of hobbits as described by Tolkien on the very opening page of the prologue to *The Lord of the Rings*: "They possessed from the first the art of disappearing swiftly and silently, when large folk whom they do not wish to meet come blundering by; and this art they have developed until to Men it may seem magical. But Hobbits have never, in fact, studied magic of any kind, and their elusiveness is due solely to a professional skill that heredity and practice, and a close friendship with the earth, have rendered inimitable by bigger and clumsier races."[2]

Clearly the gift of disappearing swiftly and silently is as natural to the hobbits as the subcreative gifts are to the elves. A good analogy would be to compare the art of disappearing swiftly and silently with similar gifts possessed by wild animals. The superior sense of hearing, eyesight, or smell that these creatures possess would indeed appear magical if humans were to possess them—as would the power of flight possessed by birds—but they are purely natural gifts these creatures possess that "bigger and clumsier" creatures do not. Similarly, the superior subcreative gifts possessed by Michelangelo, Mozart, or indeed Tolkien appear magical to those of us who do not possess such gifts. In the same way, although elven goods are superior to those made by men, the making of them is purely natural to the elves and not in the least magical, unless we are going to use the word "magical" in a very broad and loose sense applicable to wild animals, artistic geniuses, and elves.

Compare the virtuous subcreation of the elven cloaks with the vicious motives of Saruman in the weaving of his shimmering coat of many colors. Like the elven cloaks, Saruman's robes change hue with the change of light upon them, but the effect is not one of beauty but one that "bewildered" the eye of the beholder.[3] The simplicity of goodness and virtue, present in the white robes that he had formally worn, is broken into fragments, signifying his desire to break from virtue in the pursuit of relativism that claims to possess knowledge and power beyond good and evil.

Are Saruman's robes any more magical than the elven cloaks? Certainly, in one important and crucial sense, they are different in kind to anything subcreated by the elves. Saruman is, like Gandalf, one of the Maiar, angelic beings called Istari by the elves, which means "Wise Ones," but who men call wizards. His power is, therefore, supernatural and, to be more precise, demonic. Can such power be called magical? And what of the power Gandalf possesses, which we are told is "beyond the strength of kings"?[4] Can Gandalf's power be called magical? Like Saruman's, his power is supernatural, but unlike Saruman's, it is angelic and not demonic. Strictly speaking, and to ensure the necessary precision in our definitions and distinctions, Saruman's demonic power is also angelic because demons are fallen angels. What differentiates Gandalf's power from Saruman's is that Gandalf employs his supernatural gifts virtuously whereas Saruman employs his viciously. One serves the Creator and the hierarchy of creative value, the other defies the Creator, seeking to usurp the Creator's powers for prideful purposes.

We will recall, in this context, Tolkien's assertion that *The Lord of the Rings* is "an allegory . . . of *Power* (exerted for Domination)."[5] Strictly speaking, such power is not magical but miraculous, a miracle being defined as a "marvelous event due to some supernatural agency."[6] The supernatural power of God is not magical but miraculous, as is the supernatural power of his angels and saints; the supernatural power of the Devil and his demonic host is also angelic and therefore miraculous but is used—or more correctly, abused—in defiance of the giver of the gift and to usurp the order of hierarchy. Thus the demonic power of subcreation exerted and perverted by Saruman and Sauron (another more powerful demon) defies the Creator and defiles creation.

If the power of the elves is really natural and not magical, and the power of Gandalf, Sauron, and Saruman is supernatural and not magical, where, if anywhere, is magic to be found in *The Lord of the Rings*? Considering Tolkien's Catholicism and his academic grounding as a medievalist, it is not surprising that it can be found in the same sense in which it was understood and condemned by the medieval Church. Magic in Middle-earth is similar to the magic of the Middle Ages as practiced by alchemists who sought the power to turn base metal into gold in their pursuit of the philosopher's stone or who sought immortality in their pursuit of the elixir of life. The modern word for such alchemy is scientism, which can be defined as the worship of science for its power of dominance over nature. Unlike genuine science, which is an authentic path of knowledge, scientism is "power exerted for domination." Today, as in the Middle Ages, scientism is obsessed with discovering ways in which man can dominate, cheat, and defeat nature. The vast bulk of scientific research is funded by global corporations seeking ways of increasing their power through increased profits (the philosopher's stone), and the burgeoning pharmaceutical industry remains obsessed with its pursuit of the secrets of aging (the elixir of life). *Plus ça change plus c'est la même chose.* The more things change, the more they remain the same.

In this light, Tolkien's assertion that *The Lord of the Rings* is "an allegory of power (exerted for Domination)" can be seen as a reference to the magic of alchemy and scientism and their evil consequences. It is in the same light that we must also view Tolkien's additional assertion that he did not think "even Power or Domination [were] the real center" of the story, but the "real theme [was] about something much more permanent and difficult: Death and Immortality." On a theological level, this theme serves as a memento mori reminding us of death, judgment, heaven, and hell, accentuating the essential distinction between eternity and temporal longevity; on what might be termed the political level, it refers to the quest to defeat mortality in the manner in which the alchemists and the pharmacologists are seeking the elixir of life and the power over death that it brings.

The essential difference between magic in the sense in which it has just been defined and the powers of elves and wizards is that magic is neither natural nor supernatural but unnatural and antinatural. It is a war on nature. It defiles nature in its defiance of nature's laws, polluting and poisoning in its pursuit of power. It is the abuse of subcreative gifts for prideful purposes, which was encapsulated by Tolkien in *The Hobbit* in his description of the abuse of such gifts by the goblins. We are told by the narrator that "goblins are cruel, wicked, and bad-hearted" and that they "make no beautiful things, but . . . many clever ones."

> It is not unlikely that they invented some of the machines that have since troubled the world, especially the ingenious devices for killing large numbers of people at once, for wheels and engines and explosions always delighted them, and also not working with their own hands more than they could help; but in those days and those wild parts they had not advanced (as it is called) so far.[7]

In essence, therefore, it can be said that the path of virtue in Middle-earth is to live in obedience and deference to the hierarchy of creative value, reflecting it by respecting its inherent order of precedence:

1. Creator (God)
2. Creation (nature)
3. Virtuous subcreation (art and technology that reflects and respects the preceding claims of the Creator and His creation)

In contrast, the path of evil is to live in rebellion, defy-
ing the hierarchy of creative value, seeking to usurp and
invert the hierarchy's rightful order for purposes of prideful
domination:

1. Vicious subcreation (magic)
2. Creation (destroyed and polluted to serve the needs of
    magic)
3. Creator (defied, hated, and His power replaced by that of
    magic)

Once this relationship between magic and power is
understood, it can be seen that there is an inextricable
and unhealthy connection between magic and politics. It
is not surprising, therefore, that many have sought to see
The Lord of the Rings as a political allegory. Considering
that the book was being written during World War II and
the Cold War that followed in its wake, it has been sug-
gested that Mordor represents communism, Isengard represents Nazism, Gondor represents the Allied powers, and
the Shire represents an idealized vision of England. Tolkien was clearly uncomfortable with such analogizing of his
story with contemporary politics, insisting that it works on
the deeper level of theology.

Nonetheless, he does concede the legitimacy of seeing
points of applicability in his story that relate to the world
beyond the story. This being so, it must be said that the Eye
of Sauron suggests parallels with the efforts of the totalitar-
ian regimes to usurp the divine attributes of omniscience,
omnipotence, and omnipresence. In the age of secular fun-
damentalist tyranny in which *The Lord of the Rings* was

written, the leader, the Führer, was taking on godlike power, served by the all-seeing eye of the Party and its Secret Police, and striking terror into the hearts of those living in its shadow. It is perhaps no surprise that Tolkien was writing his masterpiece at the same time that George Orwell was writing *Nineteen Eighty-Four* and there are uncanny and creepy parallels between the evil eye of Big Brother and that of Tolkien's Dark Lord.

With the specter of World War II and its atrocities looming large as a backdrop to Tolkien's imagination, it is tempting to see the red eye painted on the shields of the orcs of Mordor as signifying the red flag of the communists and the white hand daubed on the shields of the Uruk-hai—Saruman's specially bred master race of storm troopers—as signifying the open-handed salute of the Nazis, as distinct from the clenched- or closed-fisted salute of the communists. An additional ominous touch of applicability is provided allusively by the fact that the hand is white—a signifier, perhaps, of the racist creed of the Nazis.

After the Ents, the very epitome of nature and tradition personified, rise up against the antinatural and "progressive" magic of Saruman, leaving his "Reich" in ruins, Gandalf and his company arrive to survey the aftermath of Isengard's defeat. Riding past the great pillar of the hand, the men of Rohan gaze upon the white hand, the symbol of Saruman's reign: "[T]he Hand appeared no longer white. It was stained as if with dried blood; and looking closer they perceived that its nails were red."[8] The staining of the hand was presumably caused by the receding flood waters, the aftermath of the Ents unleashing the cleansing force of

nature to purge Isengard of the pollution caused by Saruman's technological magic, but whatever its natural cause,
the symbolism of the bloodstained hand speaks for itself.

It would be little short of a sin of omission to conclude
this discussion of the connection between magic and politics in *The Lord of the Rings* without paying due attention to
the *palantiri.*

The *palantiri,* or seeing stones, were made by the subcreative arts of the High Elves of old and were, therefore, the
product of virtuous subcreation, but as Gandalf tells Pippin, "there is nothing that Sauron cannot turn to evil uses."[9]
Within *The Lord of the Rings,* the *palantir* stones are used by
Sauron, whose will controls them, to seduce and ultimately
dominate the mind of Saruman, and to drive Denethor, the
Steward of Minas Tirith, to despair and ultimately suicide.
It is not that the news that Saruman and Denethor receive
is completely false but that it is all one-sided. Those gazing
into the stones see only the part of the truth Sauron's will
permits them to see. In modern parlance, Sauron is feeding
his enemies propaganda so that they either are seduced to
his side, as is the case with Saruman, or are driven to the
defeatism of despair, believing the enemy is unstoppable
and destined to triumph and, in consequence, that resis-
tance is futile, as is the case with Denethor.

As a brief tangential aside, it is intriguing that Denethor is paired thematically with Théoden, both of whom
are tempted to despair through the malicious power of
misinformation. Whereas the former refuses to listen to
the wisdom of the wizard, preferring to believe the propaganda he receives from the *palantir,* the latter receives the

wizard's wisdom and exorcises the evil Wormtongue from his presence. In consequence, Denethor succumbs to suicidal despair while Théoden recovers his senses through the revival of hope.

The thematic connection is accentuated by the linguistic connection, Denethor and Théoden being near anagrams and what might be called *anaphons*—that is, phonetic "anagrams" in which the sounds of the individual syllables are rearranged. One is tempted, upon pondering this linguistic link, to wonder whether Denethor connects to paganism via Thor, the Norse god of Thunder, whereas Théoden connects to true religion via *Theos*, the Greek word for God, the root of words such as *theology*. Certainly the words of Gandalf, in rebuking Denethor for his plans to commit suicide, suggest that Tolkien had paganism in mind in his characterization of Denethor: "Authority is not given to you, Steward of Gondor, to order the hour of your death. And only the heathen kings, under the dominion of the Dark Power, did thus, slaying themselves in pride and despair, murdering their kin to ease their own death."[10] Perhaps, therefore, at the deepest level, the thematic pairing of Denethor and Théoden parallels pagan despair and Christian hope, the former engendering nihilistic defeatism and the latter inspiring the true heroism that makes victory possible.

Considering the ways the *palantiri* are used by the powers of evil to disseminate pernicious propaganda, it is intriguing that Tolkien, through the words of Gandalf, makes a point of translating the literal meaning of the word *palantir*. Gandalf informs Pippin and therefore the reader that the word means "that which looks far away."[11] More

specifically, *palantir* has its etymological roots in the Elvish
language of Quenya and consists of two elements: *palan*,
which means "far and wide," and *tir*, which means "watch."
This being so, *palantir* is often translated as simply "far-
seer." Here we see Tolkien linguistically at his most play-
ful because "far-see" in German is *Fernsehen*, the German
word for television, and indeed the word *television* itself
also means "far-see" or "far-seer." *Tele* is Greek for "far" and
video is Latin for "see."

Television was very much an ascendant technology at
the time Tolkien was writing *The Lord of the Rings*, and he
was clearly unsettled by the power that this new magic possessed to spread propaganda. In 1944, in the midst of the
writing of his epic, Tolkien wrote a letter to his son lamenting the lies being disseminated by the BBC and the Ministry
of Information,[12] the latter of which would inspire Orwell's
Ministry of Truth, the propaganda ministry in *Nineteen
Eighty-Four*. Today, more than seventy years after Tolkien
had satirized the dark magic of television, there is a deeply
ironic and wistfully whimsical lesson to be learned from
Denethor's experience as a television addict. Put bluntly
and abruptly, if we watch too much television, with its daily
dose of the Dark Lord's propaganda, we will be driven to
despair, possibly to the point of suicide.

Let's conclude our ruminations on the way magic
(vicious subcreation) is used to usurp power for the purposes of domination by reminding ourselves of where all
true power ultimately resides.

At one of the darkest moments in the story, Frodo and
Sam arrive at the Cross-Roads en route to Mordor. By the

light of the setting sun, they see the statue of an ancient king, "a huge sitting figure, still and solemn as the great stone kings of Argonath." To their horror, they see that the violent and vandalizing hands of orcs had maimed it and defaced it, defiling it with foul graffiti, "idle scrawls mixed with the foul symbols that the maggot-folk of Mordor used." The ancient statue had been decapitated, "and in its place was set in mockery a round rough-hewn stone, rudely painted by savage hands in the likeness of a grinning face with one large red eye in the midst of its forehead."[13]

The symbolism of this scene is both potent and palpable. The statue, sculpted lovingly by an ancient artist into the likeness of the king in an act of virtuous subcreation, reflects the true hierarchy of creative value. The ancient and venerable artist, like the great Michelangelo, takes a part of God's creation (the stone or marble) and raises it with a subcreative labor of love in homage to the Creator himself, of whom the king being sculpted is an authentically ordained servant. In short, the statue is a living and edifying symbol of civilization, much as Michelangelo's *Pietà* in Saint Peter's in Rome is a symbol of civilization.

If the statue is a true reflection of the hierarchy of creative value, which is the hallmark of civilization, then its defilement by the forces of darkness is a reflection of the inversion of the hierarchy, the mark of the Beast and its heathen slaves. The decapitation of the king and its replacement by an ugly and leering roughhewn stone, daubed with paint and crowned with the symbol of Sauron, signifies the triumph of the Usurper over the Creator, the turning of the order of the cosmos on its head.

And yet, in the midst of this apparent triumph of darkness over light, the light itself dispels the darkness:

> Suddenly, caught by the level beams [of the setting sun], Frodo saw the old king's head: it was lying rolled away by the roadside. "Look, Sam!" he cried, startled into speech. "Look! The king has got a crown again!"
>
> The eyes were hollow and the carven beard was broken, but about the high stern forehead there was a coronal of silver and gold. A trailing plant with flowers like small white stars had bound itself across the brows as if in reverence for the fallen king, and in the crevices of his stony hair yellow stonecrop gleamed.
>
> "They cannot conquer forever!" said Frodo. And then suddenly the brief glimpse was gone. The Sun dipped and vanished, and as if at the shuttering of a lamp, black night fell.[14]

In these few lines, as if by a miracle of grace, the hobbits have been shown a microcosmic glimpse of the order of the cosmos. As on several other occasions in both *The Hobbit* and *The Lord of the Rings*, the light of the sun (significantly capitalized in the book) is the finger of Providence—that is, the presence of the Creator himself. By his light, the power of darkness is removed so that the hobbits can be encouraged by a vision of the restoration of the true hierarchy. Thus the Creator reveals his creation, in the form of the stonecrop and the trailing plant, crowning the king and the work of art with silver and gold flowers, restoring the glory of civilization with the promise of resurrection. It

is God blessing art; it is creation crowning subcreation; it is life crowning the good, the true, and the beautiful.

Although the "brief glimpse" soon vanishes, it was, as Frodo clearly understands, the "sudden and miraculous grace" of which Tolkien writes in his essay "On Fairy-Stories," a joyous epiphany that "denies . . . universal final defeat and in so far is *evangelium*, giving a fleeting glimpse of Joy, Joy beyond the walls of the world."[15] It shows, as Sam would sing in another dark moment soon afterward, that "above all shadows rides the Sun,"[16] which is why we can be sure, as Frodo proclaims, that the powers of darkness cannot conquer forever.

CHAPTER 13

KINGS AND QUEENS

From the ashes a fire shall be woken,
A light from the shadows shall spring;
Renewed shall be blade that was broken:
The crownless again shall be king.[1]

There are two overarching formal themes that connect
and unite *The Hobbit* and *The Lord of the Rings*. The
first is the quest or rite of passage of the hobbit protagonist
(i.e., Bilbo in the former book and Frodo in the latter); the
second is the return of the king (i.e., Thorin in the former
book and Aragorn in the latter). Much has been said about
the role of the hobbits and more will be said in the following
chapters. Now, however, it is time to turn our attention to
the exiled king and his return.

It is a fact all too often overlooked that the king is more
important than the Ring as a connecting factor between
The Hobbit and *The Lord of the Rings*. In the earlier book,
the ring is merely a ring, rendered in lowercase, and not the
Ring, because there is little or no inkling of the power that

its wearer will wield in the subsequent epic. In *The Lord of the Rings*, as the power of the Ring grows and its significance increases exponentially, the shadow surrounding it darkens until it all but eclipses the relatively trivial trinket that it had been in the earlier work. In the latter book it is a perilous possession, in the former a very useful tool that is used to defeat evil and save lives.

At first sight, it would be tempting to say the same about the king in each book as we have said about the Ring. Thorin Oakenshield certainly seems a pathetic figure of a king compared with the grandeur and majesty of Aragorn. Aragorn's character and kingship are marked not only with great courage and martial prowess but also with meekness and humility and, ultimately, with the miraculous and Christlike healing power that he shows in the Paths of the Dead and the Houses of Healing.

Thorin, by comparison, is grumpy and obstreperous and falls into the destructive dragon sickness, which serves the same function in the earlier book that the gollumizing power of the Ring fulfills in *The Lord of the Rings*. Aragorn appears to be a paragon of kingly virtue, worthy of respect, reverence, and emulation; Thorin, on the other hand, seems tainted by pride and greed, and serves as a cautionary image of vice and its harmful consequences. It is true that Thorin ultimately repents and is reconciled to Bilbo but in this he resembles Boromir far more than he does Aragorn. Might we not say, therefore, that Thorin is merely a king, whereas Aragorn is a King, much as the ring in the first book is a pale shadow of the Ring in the later work?

Such a conclusion, though tempting, is erroneous because it confuses the humanity of Thorin and Aragorn with their kingship, the latter of which, as an ordained ministry, transcends their worthiness or unworthiness as men. It is for this reason that their manifold differences should not distract us from the importance of kingship or from the importance of the king's return, which serves as the fulfillment of prophecy in both books and is clearly a matter for rejoicing.

Tolkien, as a Catholic and as a medievalist, drew deep draughts of inspiration from his understanding of true kingship, particularly as manifested by legendary and historical examples of exiled kings who return to claim their rightful inheritance.

The first example of kingship, at least as it relates to Aragorn's coronation in *The Lord of the Rings*, is the figure of Charlemagne, the first Holy Roman Emperor. As the true king, Charlemagne unites all the people of Christendom just as Aragorn unites all the free peoples of Middle-earth. In this respect, those who know their medieval history—as Tolkien certainly did—will see parallels between Gandalf's role in laying the crown upon Aragorn's head, thereby bestowing the kingly authority on him, and the role of Pope Leo III in crowning Charlemagne as the Emperor in St. Peter's Basilica in Rome on Christmas Day in the year 800 A.D., which is indubitably one of the most momentous days in world history.

Long before Aragorn's coronation and shortly after Gandalf's return from the dead, we are told that "Aragorn son of Arathorn . . . looked as if some king out of the mists of the sea had stepped upon the shores of lesser men. Before him stooped the old figure, white, shining now as if with some light kindled within, bent, laden with years, but holding a power beyond the strength of kings."[2] Parallels with the pope's role in the coronation of Charlemagne are palpable. In accordance with Catholic political philosophy, authentic power, as distinct from brute power usurped for domination, resides with God and God alone, and, as such, a true king's authority needs to be authenticated by a religious service presided over by one holding the apostolic authority of the Church. It is for this reason that Charlemagne, the most powerful man in Europe, needed to be crowned by one "holding a power beyond the strength of kings."

Further evidence of the papal resonance in the characterization of Gandalf is seen in his authority to cast the disgraced Saruman from the council: "Behold, I am not Gandalf the Grey, whom you betrayed. I am Gandalf the White, who has returned from death. You have no color now, and I cast you from the order and from the Council."[3] Gandalf's reference to his return from death makes the wizard a figure of the resurrected Christ but, as we have seen, Tolkien's literary technique enables several of his characters to remind us of Christ without any of them ever being a formal allegorical personification of him. In other words, although Gandalf is meant to remind us of Christ, he is not Christ. Similarly, in his power to crown kings and excommunicate "heretics," he reminds us of the papacy without ever being a formal allegorical personification of the pope. Just as the pope, serving *in persona Christi* (i.e., in the person of Christ as his ordained minister), can grace kings with kingship, he can also "dis-grace" sinners through his powers of excommunication. Such authority comes from his position as the successor of St. Peter who, as Christ Himself ordained, has the power to bind things on earth that are thereby bound in heaven. Such power is not his, humanly speaking, but is the power of Christ working with him and through him.

Considering the suggestive papal resonance in certain aspects of Gandalf's role in the story, one can't help but wonder if the connection between his name and Castel Gandolfo—that is, Gandolf's Castle (the pope's summer residence)—is purely coincidental, as appears to have been the case with the biblical connection between Moriah and Moria and the linguistic connection between *sauros* and Sauron, or whether it is deliberate wordplay on Tolkien's part, as is the case with *lembas* and the *palantiri*.

Returning to the theme of kingship in *The Lord of the Rings*, another figure who looms large inspirationally is that of King Arthur and the Arthurian legends that surround him. Arthur is the once and future king of popular legend who hasn't really died but is only sleeping. He will return, so it is believed, in a time of great peril to deliver England from her enemies. The idea of the once and future king resonates with the person of Aragorn, the descendant of an ancient royal line who returns as a long-lost and almost forgotten king to claim his rightful inheritance and to save his kingdom from the grip of evil.

There is, however, yet another aspect of kingship that Tolkien—as a Catholic and an Englishman, understanding English history from a Catholic perspective—would have drawn upon for inspiration. This is the Jacobite

king-in-exile. Jacobites remain loyal to the heirs of the
true king of England, James II, a Catholic who was forced
into exile by the so-called Glorious Revolution of 1688. This
revolution, far from being "glorious," was, in fact, a coup
d'état in which an army of foreign mercenaries, financed
by wealthy anti-Catholic nobility, bankers, and merchants,
invaded the country to overthrow the power of the true
king. The king was forced into exile. He raised an army to
attempt to reclaim the throne but was defeated in Ireland.
In the eighteenth century, there were two Jacobite upris-
ings in which the descendants of the true king endeavored
to reclaim the throne. The second uprising, led by James's
legitimate heir, Bonnie Prince Charlie, was crushed at the
battle of Culloden in 1746. Ever since this decisive defeat,
Jacobites have lamented the passing of the Catholic mon-
archy, believing that the present incumbent on the throne
is either an usurper at worst or a steward who is keeping
the throne warm, so to speak, until the true king in exile
returns. As a devout Catholic who was steeped in the history of England, Tolkien understood all this, and there are
obvious parallels between the way a Jacobite would view
the legal status of the present royal family and the status
of Denethor as the Steward of Gondor in *The Lord of the
Rings*. From a Jacobite perspective, Queen Elizabeth II and
Denethor are both de facto rulers who hold the throne until
the return of the de jure ruler, the true king. For a Jacobite,
therefore—and it is safe to assume Tolkien had Jacobite
sympathies—the return of Aragorn would resonate with
particular poignancy. We are reminded again, perhaps, of
Tolkien's lament that as "a Christian, and indeed a Roman

Catholic . . . I do not expect 'history' to be anything but a 'long defeat'—though it contains (and in a legend may contain more clearly and movingly) some samples or glimpses of final victory."[4] In his own legend, Tolkien shows us such a glimpse in Aragorn's triumphant return.

Finally, and most importantly, we need to remind ourselves that kingship itself is only legitimate insofar as it holds its authority from God. All true kings are only true insofar as they reflect the true kingship of Christ. All lesser images, such as Aragorn's connection to Charlemagne, Arthur, or the Jacobite kings-in-exile, fall into shadow in the presence of Christ's kingship, which Aragorn's kingship reflects. In this ultimate and highest sense of kingship, the return of the king signifies the Second Coming when the "long defeat" of history will be vanquished by the final victory of Christ. This is the ultimate return from exile of the true king to claim his own.

As with Christ, Aragorn's true kingship is revealed in his miraculous ability to heal the sick. "The hands of the king are the hands of a healer," says the wise woman of Gondor, "and so shall the rightful king be known."[5] Apart from the obvious references to the healing powers of Christ in the gospel, Tolkien's love for Anglo-Saxon England would have made him well aware of the Anglo-Saxon king, St. Edward the Confessor, who was known to have such miraculous powers of healing, a fact Shakespeare alludes to in *Macbeth*, in which the true kingship of Edward the Confessor is contrasted with the murderous Machiavellianism of Macbeth. Finally, like Christ, Aragorn's power of healing extends to the dead as well as to the living. When he takes the Paths of the Dead, he reveals that he has the power to release the dead from their curse. This reminds us inescapably of Christ's descent into hell following the Crucifixion and His liberation of the dead from Limbo.

Having paid due respect to kingship in general and the kingship of Christ in particular that Tolkien exhibits in *The Lord of the Rings*, it might be well at the conclusion of this chapter to show due deference to queenship in general and to the queenship of Mary in particular that he also shows.

We have noted earlier that Tolkien cited with evident approval a critic who had seen the invocations to Elbereth and the characterization of Galadriel as "clearly related to Catholic devotion to Mary."[6] It has also been noted that the hymns of praise the elves sing to Elbereth, in which she is invoked as "Queen beyond the Western Seas" and the "Light to us that wander here,"[7] are very similar to Catholic hymns in honor of the Blessed Virgin, such as the *Salve Regina*. Such hymns do not go unheeded or unanswered in *The Lord of the Rings*. Samwise Gamgee, in his darkest hour, facing imminent death in the venomous clutches of the monstrous Shelob, is prompted to prayer by what can only be understood as miraculous grace. As he sees his death reflected in the malice of Shelob's eyes, "a thought came to him, as if some remote voice had spoken." Fumbling in his breast pocket, he feels the Phial of Galadriel:

> "Galadriel!" he said faintly, and then he heard voices far
> off but clear: the crying of the Elves as they walked under
> the stars in the beloved shadows of the Shire, and the

music of the Elves as it came through his sleep in the
Hall of Fire in the house of Elrond.

Gilthoniel A Elbereth!

And then his tongue was loosed and his voice cried in a
language which he did not know:

A Elbereth Gilthoniel

o menel palan-diriel,

le nallon si di'nguruthos!

O tiro nin, Fanuilos![8]

These Elvish words, addressed to the archangelic being
(i.e., saint), whom the elves call the Queen of the Stars, can
be translated thus:

O Elbereth, Star-Kindler

From Heaven Far-Gazing,

To thee do I cry now, 'neath Death's Shadow!

O look towards me, Everwhite!

The prayer is answered instantly as Sam, his courage and strength rekindled, staggers to his feet to face his
foe. As if in response to the hobbit's indomitable spirit,
the Phial of Galadriel blazes with its heavenly light, "like
a star that leaping from the firmament sears the dark air
with intolerable light."[9] Those with knowledge of Tolkien's
wider legendarium will know that Elbereth's face is said to
radiate the light of God (Ilúvatar) and that she is the archangel (Vala) who is most hated by Satan (Melkor). They
will also know that Shelob, Sam's foe, is a demonic spirit,

"an evil thing in spider-form,"[10] who shares Melkor's hatred of the divine light that shines from Galadriel's Phial. This broader context adds spiritual potency to Shelob's horrified response to the heavenly light blazing in the hobbit's hand: "No such terror out of heaven had ever burned in Shelob's face before. The beams of it entered into her wounded head and scored it with unbearable pain, and the dreadful infection of light spread from eye to eye. She fell back beating the air with her forelegs, her sight blasted by inner lightnings, her mind in agony."[11]

Further evidence of the role of the Virgin Mary as an inspiration to Tolkien in his writing of *The Lord of the Rings* is found in his reply to a letter from Father Robert Murray, who had written of the "positive compatibility with the order of grace" in the book and had compared the image of Galadriel to that of the Blessed Virgin. "I think I know exactly what you mean by the order of Grace," Tolkien responded, "and of course by your references to Our Lady, upon which [sic] all my own small perception of beauty both in majesty and simplicity is founded."[12] Many years later, Tolkien wrote that he was "particularly interested" by another correspondent's remarks about Galadriel: "I think it is true that I owe much of this character to Christian and Catholic teaching and imagination about Mary."[13]

Although the Marian influence on the characterization of Galadriel and the prayerful invocations to Elbereth are clear enough, it would be remiss to overlook another episode in *The Lord of the Rings* that resonates with a Catholic theological understanding of the role of Mary in salvation history. This is the moment Éowyn, the shield-maiden of

Rohan, vanquishes the Witch-king of Angmar, the Lord of
the Nazgûl. As the diminutive figure of the shield-maiden,
disguised as a male warrior, faces the might of the greatest
of Sauron's Ringwraiths, against whom even the power of
Gandalf had wavered, the Witch-king calls her a fool for
believing that she could hinder him: "Hinder me? Thou
fool. No living man may hinder me!"

"But no living man am I!" Éowyn replies. "You look
upon a woman. Éowyn I am, Éomund's daughter."[14]

The greatest of the Ringwraiths, the mightiest of Sauron's servants, seems shocked by her reply, even fearful, "as
if in sudden doubt."[15] Her words seem ominous, filled with
portents of doom, and the Witch-king's subsequent defeat
at her hands appears to be the fulfillment of an unspoken
prophecy. It's as though Éowyn's hand on the sword serves
as the hand of Providence itself.

The defeat of satanic evil by a woman, in such a manner that it is implicit that no living man but only a woman
had the power to do so, reminds Catholics of the role of
Mary as the New Eve, the one whose fidelity to God brings
forth the Savior, thereby crushing the serpent underfoot as
promised by God in the Book of Genesis.[16] Commenting on
the significance of Mary's role as the New Eve who, through
the power of God, conquers the power of Satan, Pope Benedict XVI taught the following: "At the dawn of the Creation,
Satan seems to have the upper hand, but the son of a woman
is to crush his head. Thus, through the descendence of a
woman, God himself will triumph. Goodness will triumph.
That woman is the Virgin Mary of whom was born Jesus
Christ who, with his sacrifice, defeated the ancient tempter

once and for all. This is why in so many paintings and statues of the Virgin Immaculate she is portrayed in the act of crushing a serpent with her foot."[17]

Thus as Éowyn, the diminutive shield-maiden of Rohan, crushes the serpent underfoot, we see, in the language and art of the Church Militant, which is the Church at war with the powers of darkness, an image of the Virgin most powerful (*Virgo potens*), the true shield-maiden, her babe in arms, crushing the *diabolus* with the might of her immaculate heart.

CHAPTER 14

THE THREAD OF LIFE

Now we enter the gloomiest part of the story, the trek across the wicked wastes of Mordor, the veritable Valley of Death, to Mount Doom, as ghastly as Golgotha and darker than death itself. As the shadow descends, stifling hobbit and reader alike, the darkness is lightened and the burden of foreboding is lifted by an unexpected miracle. At the foot of the dreaded mountain and bereft of all strength under the crushing weight of the Ring, Frodo crawls forward on his hands, unable to rise to his feet. Weeping in his heart, Sam resolves to carry his master, fully expecting to be crushed himself under the combined weight of Frodo and the Ring: "Sam staggered to his feet; and then to his amazement he felt the burden light. . . . Whether because Frodo was so worn by his long pains, wound of knife, and venomous sting, and sorrow, fear, and homeless wandering, or because some gift of final strength was given to him, Sam lifted Frodo with no more difficulty than if he were carrying a hobbit-child pig-a-back in some romp on the lawns or hayfields of the Shire."[1]

One scarcely knows where to start in order to unpack the multifarious moral and biblical allusions with which this one brief episode is awash. We have seen how the Ring is synonymous with sin and how wearing the Ring is equivalent to the act of sinning, the long-term addictive effect of which leads us to gollumize ourselves as we enslave ourselves to the addiction. Yet if the wearing of the Ring is the act of sinning, the carrying of it is equivalent to the carrying of the Cross or to the carrying of our own individual crosses. On one level, therefore, we can see Frodo as a Christ figure, the Cross-bearer, who saves the world from sin through his act of self-sacrifice; on another level, he is an Everyman figure, taking up his own particular cross as Christ commanded. All the while, of course, on the purely literal level, he remains merely a simple hobbit from the Shire.

But what of Sam in this analogous setting? As one who willingly bears the burden of another, struggling under the weight of evil, he can also be seen simultaneously as a Christ figure and an Everyman figure. He is doing what we are all called to do. He is taking up his own particular cross, the one that is given to him—in this case, the burden of an afflicted friend—and bears it willingly even unto death. Having done so, to his utter amazement, he finds his burden light. Notwithstanding the unconvincing "rational" reasons for this phenomenon (Frodo's pains, sorrow, and fears), we know, as Sam no doubt knows, that "some gift of final strength" has been given to him. It is, of course, a supernatural gift, a gift of grace, a miracle. It is, furthermore, a gift Christ Himself promised to those who take up their cross to follow Him: "Come to me, all you that labor, and are burdened, and I will refresh you. Take up my yoke upon you, and learn of me, because I am meek, and humble of heart: and you shall find rest to your souls. For my yoke is sweet and my burden light."[2]

Having had our burdens lifted by this unexpected lightening of the load, this miraculous spark of divine light and life, this lightning in the darkness, we are carried with Frodo to "the brink of the chasm, at the very Crack of Doom."[3] At last, after almost a thousand pages of relentless and unrelenting slog, following Frodo every inch of the way from Bag End to Mount Doom, we have finally reached the moment of victory. Now comes the easy part. All Frodo needs to do is toss the Ring into the flames below, into the maws of hell in which it was forged and to which it belongs.

If we are reading the story for the first time and have not had it spoiled for us by watching the film first or having older siblings or others tell us what happens, we are shocked, horrified, and disgusted by what happens next.

"I have come," says Frodo. "But I do not choose now to do what I came to do. I will not do this deed. The Ring is mine!"[4] Then, instead of casting the Ring into the flames, he places it on his finger.

At this point, our anger and frustration boil over: Frodo is a miserable loser! A failure! How dare he lead us through so many dangers, fraught with tension, only to let us down at the very last moment, at the absolutely crucial moment that had been the focus of all our hopes? How dare he!

Then we give the matter a little thought, and we realize it's not Frodo's fault at all. Poor Frodo had no choice in the matter. It's Tolkien's fault—he's the one with the pen. He's the one doing the writing. He's the one making the creative decisions. How dare Tolkien lead us through so many dangers, fraught with tension, only to let us down at the very last moment? How dare he!

Then we give the matter a little more thought, and it dawns on us that this twist in the plot is Tolkien's masterstroke. It is the veritable coup de grâce—in the literal sense of the word *grace*—on which the whole theological meaning of the magnum opus turns.

Frodo's failure at this crucial moment is a timely reminder that the power of evil cannot be defeated by the triumph of the will unaided by grace. From the early heresy of Pelagianism to modern day secular heresies, such as Nietzscheanism, it has been a recurring error to believe that the human will acting alone and without divine assistance (grace) can overcome the power of evil. Tolkien is no Pelagian. Still less is he a Nietzschean. Frodo is not Nietzsche's Superman, or *Übermensch*, who triumphs because of his will to power. On the contrary, he is living proof, albeit a proof brought to life in fiction, that Nietzsche's Superman, or Overman, is not only a lie but also a liar. Frodo's failure is caused by the self-delusional belief that he can become an *Übermensch* by claiming the Ring for himself. The irony that turns the joke on Nietzsche is that Frodo is fooled by the power of evil to believe that he has power over evil. It is the diabolical paradox at the darkened heart of pride of which Nietzscheanism is but one of the hydra-headed manifestations.

If there's one lesson Tolkien seeks to teach us, it is that the malicious power of the Ring possesses those who seek to possess it through the self-delusional will to power it engenders in them. It is the foolishness of selfishness.

Selfishness is to lose ourselves in the nothingness that we are without God. Selfishness is self-addiction. Selfishness gollumizes. This being so, to abandon our selfishness and give away all that belongs to our false self is to give away an illusion, the delusion of self-deception. For this reason, each of us must cast away the Ring he or she is tempted to wear. And yet we cannot cast it away without the supernatural help Christians call *grace*.

In the climactic moments on Mount Doom, with delicious and delightful irony, Frodo is saved from his selfishness and the Ring it serves by the most unlikely agent of grace imaginable. Just as he is about to turn away from the chasm in triumph—and therefore defeat—Gollum pounces upon him, bites the Ring from his finger, and falls triumphantly to his doom in the fires below, carrying the Ring with him.

This further twist in the tale beggars belief. How can we seriously believe that Gollum, a miserable sinner ruined by his addiction to the Ring, is an agent of God's grace, saving Frodo, albeit unwittingly, from sharing his own gollumized fate? The answer is found in the thread of grace woven with the hand of Providence that weaves its way throughout the story, beginning way back in the Shire and leading all the way to Mount Doom itself.

This thread of grace, which will ultimately defeat the power of the Ring and save Frodo from destruction, stretches back beyond the beginning of the story of *The Lord of the Rings* to the earlier story of *The Hobbit*. Bilbo, having discovered the Ring in the subterranean labyrinth beneath the Misty Mountains, is anxious to escape but finds his path blocked by Gollum. Concluding that he must kill the creature in order to make good his escape, Bilbo justifies his decision based on his desperate situation and the fact that Gollum had earlier intended to kill him. And yet his conscience troubles him. It would not be a fair fight. He is wearing the Ring and cannot be seen by his foe. He is also armed with a sword, whereas Gollum is unarmed. Apart from these questions of fairness or justice, there is also the question of pity or mercy toward Gollum, who is "miserable, alone, lost."

> A sudden understanding, a pity mixed with horror, welled up in Bilbo's heart: a glimpse of endless unmarked days without light or hope of betterment, hard stone, cold fish, sneaking and whispering. All these thoughts passed in a flash of a second.[5]

The moral and practical importance of this act of pity and mercy is made clear by Gandalf, ever the voice of wisdom, in response to Frodo's exclamation many years later that it was "a pity that Bilbo did not stab that vile creature, when he had the chance." "Pity?" Gandalf replies. "It was Pity that stayed his hand. Pity, and Mercy: not to strike without need. And he has been well rewarded, Frodo. Be sure that he took so little hurt from the evil, and escaped in the end, because he began his ownership of the Ring so. With Pity."[6] In these few words, we see how the pervasive role of Providence is connected to the cooperation of the individual will. It is only because Bilbo behaved virtuously

that he is ultimately able to escape. Although Gandalf appears to be referring to the long-term consequences of Bilbo's action, it is nonetheless implicit that if he had failed to act with pity and mercy, he might have perished in the struggle with Gollum or been captured and killed by the goblins that he is soon to encounter. In choosing not to take Gollum's life, Bilbo is unwittingly saving his own life and the lives of countless others in the long run.

Returning to the long-term consequences of Bilbo's act of pity and mercy, Gandalf explains to Frodo that the fate of the whole quest to destroy the Ring depended on Bilbo's passing of this primary test of virtue: "My heart tells me that [Gollum] has some part to play yet, for good or ill, before the end: and when that comes, the pity of Bilbo may rule the fate of many—yours not least."[7] As the unfolding of subsequent events proves, Gandalf's words are those of a prophet. They are also words that Tolkien wants to ensure the reader, as well as Frodo, remembers because they are repeated almost verbatim when Frodo and Sam are debating what to do with Gollum after they capture him. As Frodo ponders whether they should kill him, justifying such a course of action on the basis that Gollum plans to kill them if he has the opportunity, he hears, "quite plainly but far off, voices out of the past."

> What a pity Bilbo did not stab the vile creature, when he had a chance!
>
> Pity? It was Pity that stayed his hand. Pity, and Mercy: not to strike without need.[8]

"Very well," Frodo answers out loud, lowering his sword at the prompting of the voices reverberating in his memory.

"But still I am afraid. And yet, as you see, I will not touch the creature. For now that I see him, I do pity him."[9]

It is intriguing that Frodo's words, even if he is merely thinking out loud, are addressed to Gandalf, whom he believes is dead and whose death he witnessed. In any event, regardless of whether we wish to view Frodo's words to the wizard as a prayer to the dead or whether we choose to dismiss them as merely piously phrased thoughts addressed to the insubstantial ghosts of his past, the words are potent with importance because they are portentous of Gandalf's prophecy that Gollum has some part to play yet before the end and that the fate of many will depend on the pity shown to him.

In the same manner that Bilbo passes the hardest of tests, that of loving his enemy, Frodo likewise acts virtuously, showing pity and mercy in the face of formidable temptation, thereby leaving the life-giving thread unbroken.

Sometime later, at the Forbidden Pool, Anborn, one of the men in Faramir's company, has Gollum at arrow point, poised to shoot.

"Shall we shoot?" Faramir asks.

"No!" Frodo exclaims. "No! I beg you not to."

Faramir asks why the creature should be spared and Frodo responds that Gollum is "wretched and hungry, and unaware of his danger." Apart from such pity being enough to stay the archer's hand, Frodo calls on the ghost of Gandalf to plead on Gollum's behalf, reminding us of the prophecy: "And Gandalf, your Mithrandir, he would have bidden you not to slay him for that reason, and for others. He forbade the Elves to do so. I do not know clearly why, and of what I guess I cannot speak openly out here. But this creature is in some way bound up with my errand."[10] Persuaded by Frodo's words and by Gandalf's plea by proxy, Faramir spares Gollum and leaves the crucial thread unbroken.

Bilbo and Frodo having now passed the test of loving their enemy, the final test falls on the shoulders of Sam, who had earlier echoed Frodo's complaint that it was a pity Gollum had not been killed. On the slopes of Mount Doom, he finds the creature at his mercy. "Now!" he cries. "At last I can deal with you!" As he advances on Gollum with a drawn sword, the creature begs for his life. Sam's hand wavers. Hot with anger and knowing that Gollum had been treacherous and had planned to murder him and his master, he feels that the shriveled, shrunken heap at his feet deserves to die and that his death would remove the threat he posed to Frodo's life. "But deep in his heart there was something that restrained him: he could not strike this thing lying in the dust, forlorn, ruinous, utterly wretched. He himself, though only for a little while, had borne the Ring, and now dimly guessed the agony of Gollum's shrivelled mind and body, enslaved to that Ring, unable to find peace or relief ever in life again."[11] Like his master and Bilbo before him, Sam stays his hand and shows Gollum pity and mercy. Thus, at the last, as the whole future of Middle-earth hung quite literally on an invisible thread of life, Sam's virtuous choice to love his enemy ruled the fate of many.

Two pages later, Gollum plunges into the maws of Mount Doom, clutching the Ring triumphantly as they plummet to their destruction. "Out of the depths came his last wail *Precious*, and he was gone."[12]

What are we to make of Gollum's final moments, which seem, from his perspective, to constitute a happy ending? He has what he wants—indeed, he has the only thing that he wants, or at least the only thing that he thinks he wants. His personal quest to once more possess the Ring and be possessed by it has been achieved. Should we be as saddened by Gollum's success as we are angered by Frodo's failure, or should we rejoice that he finally got what he wanted, even if what he wanted was Hell itself?

The first thing we need to understand is that Tolkien's theological perspective, and the deep psychology that springs from it, is profoundly orthodox. In the same manner in which Frodo's subjective failure is an objective success, in the sense that the error that springs from his final weakness is rectified by the providential thread of life that rewards his earlier acts of virtue, so Gollum's subjective success is an objective failure: in getting what he thinks he wants, he loses what he really wants—whether he thinks he wants it or not—which is the peace that comes from being free of his addiction to evil.

The other thing we need to know is that Tolkien's theological understanding of the Four Last Things—Death, Judgment, Heaven and Hell—is also profoundly orthodox. God doesn't send people to Heaven or Hell. Those in Heaven are there because they want to be; those in Hell are there because they want to be. God merely respects the freedom of the human will to choose where it wishes to spend eternity. Do we choose to lose the nothingness that we are without God by choosing to become the something that we are meant to be with him, a process of selfless sanctification that is the ultimate purpose and meaning of life, or do we choose ourselves above all else and the addiction to ourselves that it entails? Gollum chose the latter and gets the desire of his addicted heart, which chooses to be enslaved eternally to itself. (Admirers of C. S. Lewis will no doubt see similarities between Gollum's choice and that of the infernal souls in Lewis's eschatological parable, *The Great Divorce*.)

Returning to our earlier question regarding how we should feel about Gollum's final resting place, the answer is given to us by Frodo. Responding to Sam's statement that Gollum had "gone now beyond recall, gone forever," Frodo suspends final judgment with words of forgiveness that also serve as a reminder of the providential thread of life that bound all three of them together: "Yes," he says. "But do you remember Gandalf's words: *Even Gollum may have something yet to do?* But for him, Sam, I could not have destroyed the Ring. The Quest would have been in vain, even at the bitter end. So let us forgive him! For the Quest is achieved, and now all is over."[13]

If Gollum's tragic end serves the greater end of destroying the power of evil, can we perhaps gain at least a modicum of consolation and even a degree of satisfaction that justice is done? Perhaps indeed we can. But what about pity and mercy, not to judge too hastily or without need? Should we not be haunted by Gandalf's rebuke to Frodo at the beginning of the quest?

"I can't understand you," Frodo had said. "Do you mean to say that you, and the Elves, have let him live on after all those horrible deeds? Now at any rate he is as bad as an Orc, and just an enemy. He deserves death."

"Deserves it!" Gandalf had exclaimed. "I daresay he does. Many that live deserve death. And some that die deserve life. Can you give it to them? Then do not be too eager to deal out death in judgement. For even the very wise cannot see all ends."

Isn't the Frodo who forgives Gollum at the end of the quest a little closer to heaven than the one who had condemned him at its beginning?

After all is said and done, after the proud have been humiliated and the humble have been exalted, the quest resolves itself into a question that the quest has answered: Isn't it sufficient to know that Frodo's failure and Gollum's success are bound together in a golden thread of grace, which is more powerful than the Ring and all its servants?

It is indeed sufficient, and we have the quest to thank for answering the question.

CHAPTER 15

HEAVEN HAVEN

I have desired to go
Where springs not fail,
To fields where flies no sharp and sided hail,
And a few lilies blow.
And I have asked to be
Where no storms come,
Where the green swell is in the havens dumb,
And out of the swing of the sea.

—Gerard Manley Hopkins,
"Heaven Haven."

There is an inevitable sense of anticlimax attached to the final chapters of *The Lord of the Rings*. The dramatic culmination of the quest on the brink of the abyss above the fires of Mount Doom was the consummation of all the hopes that we, as readers, had invested in the story. After the exhilaration of the moment and the exhalation of the sigh of contented relief that followed in its wake, there seems little point in going on. We are inclined to drag our

feet for the remainder of the story, basking in the afterglow
of the Ring's destruction but not knowing where, if anywhere, the plot still has to go. And yet we are reminded
by Gandalf that the end of the Ring's power is also a new
beginning for Middle-earth. Two weeks after the destruction of the Ring, Gandalf tells Sam, "[I]n Gondor the New
Year will always now begin upon the twenty-fifth of March
when Sauron fell, and when you were brought out of the
fire to the King."[1]

And so it is that Tolkien plants the clue that, as we discovered and discussed in chapter 3, unlocks the deepest
theological meaning at the Catholic heart of the work. As
with the Annunciation and the Crucifixion, both of which
happened historically on March 25, the date evil is over-
thrown in Middle-earth marks a new beginning. With
even greater subtlety, Tolkien buries a further important
clue in the appendices to the story. In Appendix B, he
discloses that the Fellowship of the Ring leaves Rivendell
on December 25,[2] drawing a symbolic parallel between
Frodo's journey and the life of Christ. Having formally
taken on the burden of the Ring, his "Christmas present" in ironic contrast to Gollum's "birthday present," at
the Council of Elrond, Frodo sets out from Rivendell on
the birthday of Jesus and journeys under the increasing
weight of the Ring until he arrives at Mount Doom (Golgotha) on the historic date of the Crucifixion. In this symbolic sense, the Ring, which we have already seen as being
symbolic of sin, is also seen to be a symbol of the Cross.
By extension, Frodo, as the Cross-bearer journeying from
Christmas Day to Good Friday under the increasing

weight of sin, emerges as a veritable figure of Christ, and it is in this context that his role in Aragorn's coronation is to be understood.

To everyone's surprise, Aragorn does not place the crown on his own head but requests that the Ring-bearer bring the crown to him and that Gandalf should set it upon his head.[3] We have already discussed the connection between Aragorn and Charlemagne and the significance, in this context, of Gandalf being a figure of the pope in his placing of the crown on the king's head, as Pope Leo III had placed the crown on the head of Charlemagne. We also discussed the tenets of Catholic philosophy, which holds that all political authority comes from Christ, not "the people," and that the pope's crowning of Charlemagne was deemed necessary to show Charlemagne's authentic—that is, God-given—right to rule. The pope had the authority to do this because, as the successor of St. Peter, he had been given authority to bind on earth things that would be bound in heaven.

His power is, however, never his own but is the power of Christ working with him and through him. In this sense, the crown that Christ bestows upon the pope gives him the authority to bestow the crown upon temporal kings and emperors. Once this hierarchical order of authority is understood, we can see that Frodo as the Ring-bearer (Cross-bearer) is the figure of Christ who hands the crown to Gandalf (pope figure) who then sets it upon the head of the king (temporal ruler). Regardless of whether one is comfortable with Catholic political philosophy, Tolkien is clearly endorsing it in the symbolism he employs for the coronation of Aragorn, a fact that is reinforced by the grace and power the religious ritual has apparently bestowed upon him: "But when Aragorn arose all that beheld him gazed in silence, for it seemed to them that he was revealed to them now for the first time . . . wisdom sat upon his brow, and strength and healing were in his hands, and a light was about him."[4]

Leaving the pomp and circumstance of Gondor for the agrarian simplicity of the Shire, the returning hobbits are horrified to discover that the fallout from the macrocosmic struggle in which they had been embroiled has affected and infected their beloved homeland. Industrialism has taken a vicelike grip on the land, polluting it with dark satanic mills and bringing with it the big and intrusive government that always accompanies big and intrusive business. The scouring of the Shire, which restores the hobbit-folk to their senses, is a further manifestation of Tolkien's deeply rooted Catholicism, in this case his adherence to Catholic social teaching and its advocacy of subsidiarity and the sort of sane alternatives to the rule of Mammon advocated by Catholic thinks, such as Hilaire Belloc and G. K. Chesterton, both of whom were significant influences on Tolkien in his formative years. In many respects, the chapter of *The Lord of the Rings* entitled "The Scouring of the Shire" can be seen as a distributist parable in the spirit of Chesterton's novel, *The Napoleon of Notting Hill.*

After all is set right in the Shire, what remains, especially for Frodo, is a sense of exile from what Chesterton calls "that home behind home for which we are all homesick."[5] In Christian terms, this is the desire for heaven which, as St. Thomas Aquinas said, is "our true native land."[6] We have already discussed how this homesickness for the true home beyond our reach, this sense of exile from our true native land, is what animates the hymns of the elves, echoing Catholic hymns referring to this life as a place of banishment, a "vale of tears," and a land of exile.

For the elves, the desire that Christians feel toward heaven is felt toward the Undying Lands, a realm beyond the reach of mortals but attainable for those elves who make the journey into the mystic west. Parallels with a Christian view of the afterlife are exemplified by lines from St. Thomas Aquinas's Corpus Christi sequence in which the saint rejoices in the good things to be seen in "the land of the living," a pretty close approximation to "the undying lands."

Such parallels, inextricably connected to Tolkien's own Catholic spirituality, help us understand the way *The Lord of the Rings* ends. Frodo, like the elves, feels a deep sense of exile and restlessness, even homelessness. It is, therefore, a consummation of a deep-seated need and desire that he accompanies Elrond, Galadriel, Gandalf, and Bilbo on the voyage to the Undying Lands, the two hobbits exempted from the usual ban on mortals making the voyage on account of the honor due to them as Ring-bearers.

Following the tear-laden farewells to his hobbit companions Sam, Merry, and Pippin, Frodo bids farewell to Middle-earth and sails into the sunset toward a land beyond death: "[A]t last on a night of rain Frodo smelled a sweet fragrance on the air and heard the sound of singing

that came over the water. And then it seemed to him that as in the dream in the house of Bombadil, the grey rain-curtain turned all to silver glass and was rolled back, and he beheld white shores and beyond them a far green country under a swift sunrise."[7]

Returning to the imagery of the *Salve Regina*, it's as though the grey rain curtain being rolled back is the veil of tears being removed so that the fully healed Frodo can behold what Gerard Manley Hopkins has called "the heaven-haven of the reward."[8]

This is a happy ending indeed but Tolkien doesn't allow us the comfort or luxury of such an ending. The story doesn't conclude with Frodo's sudden glimpse of heaven but with Sam's melancholy return home to his wife and daughter: "And there was yellow light, and fire within; and the evening meal was ready, and he was expected. And Rose drew him in, and set him in his chair, and put little Elanor upon his lap. He drew a deep breath. 'Well, I'm back,' he said."[9]

Why does Tolkien choose to end his epic in such an anticlimactic and even melancholic manner? Why not leave us with Frodo's vision of the paradise beyond death? The answer is simple if somewhat sobering. He leaves us where he found us, stranded in the long defeat and living with our sense of exile: "Actually I am a Christian, and indeed a Roman Catholic, so that I do not expect 'history' to be anything but a 'long defeat'—though it contains (and in a legend may contain more clearly and movingly) some samples or glimpses of final victory."[10]

He leaves us *where* he found us, but he doesn't leave us *how* he found us. We are not as we were when we set out on the journey with Frodo and Sam all those many pages earlier. We are changed as they are changed. In discovering the hidden meaning of *The Lord of the Rings*, we are discovering one of the most sublime and astonishing glimpses of the final victory that has ever been shown in the long and troubled history of man. For this, as for so much else, we owe a great debt of gratitude to J. R. R. Tolkien.

NOTES

CHAPTER ONE

1. Humphrey Carpenter, ed., *The Letters of J. R. R. Tolkien* (New York: Houghton Mifflin, 2000), p. 172.
2. J. R. R. Tolkien, foreword to *The Lord of the Rings*, 2nd ed. (New York: Houghton Mifflin, 2004), pp. xxiii–xxiv.
3. Carpenter, ed., *Letters of J. R. R. Tolkien*, p. 246.
4. G. K. Chesterton, *Orthodoxy*, 5th ed. (London: The Bodley Head, 1915), p. 85.
5. Ibid., pp. 108–10.
6. Although written by Wilde, these words are actually spoken by the character Lord Darlington in act 3 of *Lady Windermere's Fan*.
7. C. S. Lewis, *The Voyage of the Dawn Treader* (New York: Harper Trophy, 2005), p. 226.
8. Tolkien, *Lord of the Rings*, p. 909.
9. J. R. R. Tolkien, *Tree and Leaf* (London: Unwin, 1988), p. 56.
10. Ibid., p. 28.
11. Ibid., p. 69.
12. Ibid., p. 28.

CHAPTER TWO

1. Carpenter, ed., *Letters of J. R. R. Tolkien*, p. 288.
2. Ibid.
3. Ibid., pp. 288–89.
4. Tolkien, *Tree and Leaf*, p. 69.

CHAPTER THREE

1. Martin C. D'Arcy, *Laughter and the Love of Friends: Reminiscences of the Distinguished English Priest and Philosopher* (Westminster, MD: Christian Classics, 1991), pp. 112–13.
2. It should, however, be noted that Tolkien was an expert on the Anglo-Saxon language and its literature and was not, as Father D'Arcy seemed to believe, a historian.
3. The Pelagians believed that men could forge their own eternal destiny, earning themselves a place in heaven by obeying the teachings of Christ through a triumph of the human will over temptation. Such a belief denied the need for grace and therefore denied the need for the Church and her sacraments.
4. There is much disagreement about the exact dating of *Beowulf*, its composition being shrouded in mystery. The present author agrees with those, including Tolkien, who believe it was written sometime between the mid-seventh and mid-eighth century.
5. All quotes from *Beowulf* are from Seamus Heaney's translation, *Beowulf* (New York: W. W. Norton & Company, 2002)
6. For the sake of clarity, Chaucer's original English has been modified. The purist, I hope, will forgive me.

CHAPTER FOUR

1. Tolkien, *Lord of the Rings*, pp. 33–34.

2. Ibid., p. 46.
3. Mt 6:21.
4. Tolkien, *Lord of the Rings*, p. 47.
5. Ibid., p. 222.

CHAPTER FIVE

1. Chesterton, *Orthodoxy*, p. 108.
2. Tolkien, *Lord of the Rings*, p. 56.
3. J. R. R. Tolkien, *The Hobbit* (London: HarperCollins, 1988), p. 285.
4. Tolkien, *Lord of the Rings*, p. 55.
5. Ibid.
6. Ibid., p. 56.
7. G. K. Chesterton, letter to Maurice Baring; quoted in Emma Letley, *Maurice Baring: A Citizen of Europe* (London: Constable, 1991), p. 217.
8. Tolkien, *Lord of the Rings*, p. 59.
9. Ibid.

CHAPTER SIX

1. Carpenter, ed., *Letters of J. R. R. Tolkien*, p. 174.
2. Ibid., p. 26.
3. Ibid., p. 192.
4. Tolkien, *Lord of the Rings*, p. 131.
5. Ibid., pp. 131–32.
6. Ibid., pp. 132–33.
7. Gn 2:19.

CHAPTER SEVEN

1. Carpenter, ed., *Letters of J. R. R. Tolkien*, p. 246.
2. Ibid., p. 255.

3. Tolkien, *Lord of the Rings*, p. 357.

4. Ibid., p. 87.

5. Ibid., p. 79.

6. Ibid., p. 80.

7. In the final line of his Eucharistic hymn *Verbum supernum prodiens*, the last two stanzas of which form the shorter and better-known Eucharistic hymn, *O Salutaris Hostia*.

8. *Morgoth's Ring*, one of the volumes in Christopher Tolkien's *History of Middle-Earth*, illustrates how Tolkien's Christian cosmology inspired and informed the cosmology of Middle-earth.

9. Tolkien, *Lord of the Rings*, p. 357.

10. Ibid., p. 243.

11. Ibid., p. 244.

12. J. R. R. Tolkien, *The Silmarillion* (New York: Ballantine Books, 2002), p. 36.

CHAPTER EIGHT

1. Tolkien, *Lord of the Rings*, p. 398.

2. Ibid., p. 671.

3. Ibid., p. 613.

4. Ibid., pp. 258–89.

5. Sauron is described as the greatest of Melkor's servants. Melkor is quite clearly and inescapably the name that the elves have ascribed in their own creation myth to Satan. Tolkien, *Silmarillion*, p. 23.

6. Tolkien, *Lord of the Rings*, pp. 399–400.

7. Ibid., p. 414.

8. Ibid., p. 671.

9. Ibid., p. 664.

10. Jn 8:34.

11. Rom 6:18–20.

CHAPTER NINE

1. Carpenter, ed., *Letters of J. R. R. Tolkien*, p. 288.
2. Ibid.
3. Ibid., pp. 274–75.
4. Tolkien, *Lord of the Rings*, p. 936.
5. Glenn Dallaire, "Miracle of the Eucharist," *Miracles of the Saints*, accessed November 30, 2014, http://www.miracles ofthesaints.com/2010/10/miracle-of-eucharist-total-fast -from.html#sthash.KIYDQuqq.dpuf.
6. Tolkien, *Lord of the Rings*, pp. 369–70.
7. Carpenter, ed., *Letters of J. R. R. Tolkien*, p. 288.

CHAPTER TEN

1. Tolkien, *Lord of the Rings*, p. 306.
2. Ibid., p. 308.
3. Mt 18: 3–4.
4. Tolkien, *Lord of the Rings*, p. 330.
5. Tolkien, *Silmarillion*, p. 15.
6. Ibid., p. 9.
7. Gn 1:1–3.
8. Clyde S. Kilby, *Tolkien & The Silmarillion* (Chicago: Harold Shaw, 1976), p. 59.
9. Carpenter, ed., *Letters of J. R. R. Tolkien*, p. 201.
10. Ibid., p. 202.
11. Strictly speaking, this is a theological flaw because angels, having made the once-and-for-all decision to serve God or Satan, do not change sides. Angels are always angelic (i.e., good); demons are always demonic (i.e., evil).
12. Carpenter, ed., *Letters of J. R. R. Tolkien*, p. 202.
13. Gn 22:2.
14. Carpenter, ed., *Letters of J. R. R. Tolkien*, p. 383.
15. Tolkien, *Lord of the Rings*, p. 495.

16. Ibid.
17. G. K. Chesterton, *The Ballad of the White Horse* (London: Methuen, 1928), p. 140.
18. Tolkien, *Tree and Leaf*, p. 62.
19. Carpenter, ed., *Letters of J. R. R. Tolkien*, p. 100.

CHAPTER ELEVEN

1. Tolkien, *Lord of the Rings*, pp. 496–97.
2. Ibid., p. 595.
3. Ibid., p. 585.
4. Ibid., p. 729.
5. Ibid., p. 520.
6. Gn 3:14.
7. Tolkien, *Lord of the Rings*, p. 520.
8. Tolkien, *Silmarillion*, p. 8.
9. Ibid., p. 10.
10. Ibid., p. 23.
11. Isa 14:11–12.
12. Tolkien, *Silmarillion*, p. 23.
13. Ibid., pp. 23–24.
14. Carpenter, ed., *Letters of J. R. R. Tolkien*, p. 380.
15. J. R. R. Tolkien, *Morgoth's Ring* (Boston: Houghton Mifflin, 1993), pp. viii–ix.
16. Ibid., p. ix.
17. Tolkien, *Lord of the Rings*, p. 909.
18. Tolkien, *Silmarillion*, p. 6.
19. Ibid.
20. Tolkien, *Lord of the Rings*, p. 702.

CHAPTER TWELVE

1. Tolkien, *Lord of the Rings*, p. 370.
2. Ibid., p. 1.

3. Ibid., p. 259.

4. Ibid., p. 501.

5. Carpenter, ed., *Letters of J. R. R. Tolkien*, p. 246.

6. *Concise Oxford Dictionary*, 5th ed., 1963.

7. Tolkien, *Hobbit*, p. 69.

8. Tolkien, *Lord of the Rings*, p. 555.

9. Ibid., p. 583.

10. Ibid., p. 853.

11. Ibid.

12. Carpenter, ed., *Letters of J. R. R. Tolkien*, p. 93.

13. Tolkien, *Lord of the Rings*, p. 702.

14. Ibid.

15. Tolkien, *Tree and Leaf*, p. 62.

16. Tolkien, *Lord of the Rings*, p. 909.

CHAPTER THIRTEEN

1. Tolkien, *Lord of the Rings*, p. 247.

2. Ibid., p. 501.

3. Ibid., p. 583.

4. Carpenter, ed., *Letters of J. R. R. Tolkien*, p. 255.

5. Tolkien, *Lord of the Rings*, p. 862.

6. Carpenter, ed., *Letters of J. R. R. Tolkien*, p. 288.

7. Tolkien, *Lord of the Rings*, p. 79.

8. Ibid., p. 729.

9. Ibid., p. 730.

10. Ibid., p. 723.

11. Ibid., p. 730.

12. Carpenter, ed., *Letters of J. R. R. Tolkien*, pp. 171–72.

13. Ibid., p. 407.

14. Tolkien, *Lord of the Rings*, p. 841.

15. Ibid.

16. Gn 3:15.

17. Benedict XVI, Angelus Address, December 8, 2009.

CHAPTER FOURTEEN

1. Tolkien, *Lord of the Rings*, p. 941.
2. Mt 11:28–30.
3. Tolkien, *Lord of the Rings*, p. 945.
4. Ibid.
5. Tolkien, *Hobbit*, p. 90.
6. Tolkien, *Lord of the Rings*, p. 59.
7. Ibid.
8. Ibid., p. 615.
9. Ibid.
10. Ibid., pp. 684–86.
11. Ibid., p. 944.
12. Ibid., p. 946.
13. Ibid., p. 947.

CHAPTER FIFTEEN

1. Tolkien, *Lord of the Rings*, p. 952.
2. Ibid., p. 1092.
3. Ibid., pp. 967–68.
4. Ibid., p. 968.
5. G. K. Chesterton, *The New Jerusalem* (New York: George H. Doran, 1921), p. 50.
6. In the final words of his hymn, *O Salutaris Hostia*.
7. Tolkien, *Lord of the Rings*, p. 1030.
8. In the final stanza of Hopkins, "The Wreck of the Deutschland."
9. Tolkien, *Lord of the Rings*, p. 1031.
10. Carpenter, ed., *Letters of J. R. R. Tolkien*, p. 255.

INDEX

About the Author

Joseph Pearce is Director of the Center for Faith and Culture and Writer in Residence at Aquinas College in Nashville, Tennessee. He is a renowned biographer whose books include his autobiography, *Race with the Devil: My Journey from Racial Hatred to Rational Love* (Saint Benedict Press, 2013); *Candles in the Dark: The Authorized Biography of Fr. Ho Lung, Missionaries of the Poor* (Saint Benedict Press, 2012); *Through Shakespeare's Eyes: Seeing the Catholic Presence in the Plays* (Ignatius Press, 2010); and *Tolkien: Man and Myth, a Literary Life* (HarperCollins, 1998). He is the recipient of an Honorary Doctorate of Higher Education from Thomas More College for the Liberal Arts and also received the Pollock Award for Christian Biography. He is co-editor of the *St. Austin Review* and has hosted two series on Shakespeare for EWTN, as well as hosting several EWTN productions on J. R. R. Tolkien.

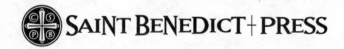